THE FORTUNE TELLER'S
MAH JONGG

THE ANCIENT GAME AS A MODERN ORACLE

DEREK WALTERS

CARDS ILLUSTRATED BY AMANDA BARLOW

VIKING
STUDIO
BOOKS

VIKING STUDIO BOOKS
Published by the Penguin Group
Penguin Books USA Inc., 375 Hudson Street,
New York, New York 10014, U.S.A.
Penguin Books Ltd, 27 Wrights Lane,
London W8 5TZ, England
Penguin Books Australia Ltd, Ringwood,
Victoria, Australia
Penguin Books Canada Ltd, 10 Alcorn Avenue,
Toronto, Ontario, Canada M4V 3B2
Penguin Books (N.Z.) Ltd, 182–190 Wairau Road,
Auckland 10, New Zealand

Penguin Books Ltd, Registered Offices:
Harmondsworth, Middlesex, England

This edition published in 1994 by Viking Penguin,
a division of Penguin Books USA Inc.

10 9 8 7 6 5 4 3 2 1

Text copyright © Derek Walters, 1988
Illustrations copyright © Eddison Sadd Editions, 1988
This edition copyright © Eddison Sadd Editions, 1988

AN EDDISON · SADD EDITION
Edited, designed and produced by
Eddison Sadd Editions Limited
St Chad's Court, 146B King's Cross Road, London WC1X 9DH

CIP data available
ISBN 0–670–85640–1

Phototypeset by Bookworm Typesetting, Manchester, England
Origination of cards by Columbia Offset, Singapore
Printed and bound in China
Produced by Mandarin Offset

CONTENTS

THE
ORACLE

占卜

The Origins of the Oracle

In China, the professional soothsayer is held in great reverence. The calling is a dignified one, and does not attract the sort of suspicion that it does in the western world, where 'fortune-tellers' are regarded at best with amusement, at worst hostility, and generally, with tolerant scepticism.

Throughout the Far East, many of the major temples have their own diviners attached, and the most celebrated of them support a considerable staff of soothsayers to minister to the faithful each day of the week. For millions of people divination is actually an integral part of their worship.

Within the temples themselves, the oracles used are elementary enough. The most basic is the *Kao Pui*: the enquirer takes two curved blocks, which are thrown on the ground three times to elicit a straightforward 'yes' or 'no'. (These are likely to be similar, if not identical, to the 'urim and thummim' mentioned in the Bible.) The other well-known temple oracle uses bamboo sticks, each bearing a number, which is then interpreted by one of the resident priests or diviners in attendance.

But beyond the temple precincts, however, there are vast numbers of ways by which the uncertain future may be revealed. Sometimes recourse is made to a professional astrologer, but as this usually involves an exorbitant fee it is a considerable asset if one of the elders of the family is adept at the *Ya Pai Shen Po* – literally, 'divination by ivory blocks' - by which the Chinese understand dominoes, cards, or Mah Jongg tiles.

The modern game of Mah Jongg is actually a direct descendant of an ancient oracle that was consulted by Chinese soothsayers thousands of years ago. When Chinese astronomers first began to record the progress of the Sun, Moon and planets they used a simple device – a divining board – to calculate the expected positions of the heavenly bodies. Their progress through the skies was recorded by moving counters round the divisions of the board. In the course of time this primitive planisphere was adapted into a board game which would be readily recognizable today as ludo; later, the dice used in the game evolved into dominoes, and then, when the Chinese invented printing, the domino patterns were transferred to cards. So it was that an ancient oracle came to be the ancestor of virtually all our present indoor games from poker to Monopoly.

In the west the mystical origins of cards, dominoes and dice have been all but forgotten, except by the Mah Jongg player who is constantly reminded of the game's dignified ancestry in the ritual preparation for play, the affectionate names for some of the pieces, and the technical terms used for strategies and tactics of the game.

Introduction to the Mah Jongg Oracle
After many years of experience with the Mah Jongg oracle, I have come to find that its predictions are uncannily accurate, while the advice it proffers is practical, sound, and specific.

Unfortunately, the ivory and bamboo sets, beautiful as they are to handle, are at once cumbersome and expensive, while the would-be novice is often deterred by the Chinese inscriptions. The aim of these present Mah Jongg oracle cards has been to preserve the signals and symbols of the original oracles in a much more accessible way, by being convenient and easy to understand, but without losing any of the beauty or mystery of the original.

The Symbolism of Mah Jongg

When Chinese gamblers set out their ivory and bamboo Mah Jongg tiles, they are about to embark on a game which, because of its unique scoring system, may end with the players losing or gaining fortunes. It is no wonder, therefore, that the game reflects so many ancient Chinese philosophical principles. Instead of merely dealing out tiles to each player, there is a traditional ritual of building four walls of tiles, like the boundaries of an ancient Chinese city. The square formed by the four walls is the symbol of the Earth. The four sides are termed East, South, West and North, but not according to terrestrial directions: West and East are reversed in relation to North and South, for the playing area is a celestial map, not an earthly one.

The four directions are each matched by the four tiles usually known as the Four Winds. Naturally, it is regarded as very fortunate when the tile of a particular direction appears in its appropriate place. The four directions match the four seasons of the year; the Sun rising in the East signifies the beginning of the year, hence, Spring; the Sun is in the South at its highest point during the day, suggesting Summer; it sets in the West, which accordingly represents Autumn, and neglects the North, which is therefore cold, so symbolizing Winter.

In Mah Jongg, the four seasons are represented in the pack by two sets of four tiles bearing pictures symbolizing the seasons, either by showing an appropriate flower, or by some seasonal occupation. Together, these eight tiles represent the Eight Immortals: guardians who guide and protect those under their care. They also represent the eight trigrams of the I *Ching* – perhaps the most ancient divination system on record.

However, Chinese philosophers actually reckon that there are five cardinal points, by considering the Centre, from which the four directions radiate, to be one of them. Accordingly, among the Mah Jongg tiles is one representing the fifth, stationary direction, although this is usually called the Red Dragon by westerners, unaware of its significance.

These five cardinal points represent the five elements of Chinese theory – Wood, Fire, Earth, Metal and Water. (The order of the five elements can be remembered by recalling that Wood burns, making Fire, leaving an earthy ash; the Earth yields Metal, which can be melted into a liquid, like Water.) The Chinese are extremely fond of classifying everything into fives, according to their association with the five elements; thus there are (according to the Chinese) five senses, five tastes, five viscera, five epochs, and so forth. Astrologers associate the five elements with the five major planets: Jupiter, Mars, Saturn, Venus and Mercury.

The attributes of the five elements match the five directions; thus East, the Spring, associated with Wood, represents growing things, birth, creativity, and peace, while conversely the West is associated with Autumn, Metal, old age, reaping, and military conflicts. Note the curious difference between Chinese and Western astrology; the Chinese associate the Metal planet (Venus) with the masculine, and the Wood planet (Jupiter) with the feminine.

Finally, it is worth remarking that the number of tiles dealt to each player in the game of Mah Jongg, and used in divination, is thirteen, which is the number of lunar months in the solar year.

The Cards Used in Mah Jongg

The exceptionally large number of cards used in Mah Jongg – almost double the number in the Tarot – always appears bewildering at first. But fortunately the matter is nowhere nearly as complicated as it might appear.

The complete Mah Jongg set actually comprises four identical decks each of thirty-four cards, plus eight separate 'Guardian' cards, which are easily distinguished from the cards in the four decks by a coloured border.

The four decks can be further divided into the Honours and Suits, there being seven honours cards and twenty-seven suit cards – three suits of nine cards each – making thirty-four cards in each pack.

The four packs of thirty-four cards, together with the eight non-repeated Guardian cards, make a total of 144 cards. (In addition to the cards described above, three blank cards are included in the set to replace any which might get mislaid. These should be removed and put safely to one side as being of no immediate use.)

The traditional design of the Mah Jongg playing tile is shown in the upper right-hand corner of the oracle cards. As the design of the suit cards is closest to those of Western playing cards, it is convenient to describe these first.

The Three Suits

The three suits are Bamboo, Circles and Wan (meaning 'ten thousands'). Wan are sometimes called 'Characters' by Mah Jongg players. With the exception of one card, 1 Bamboo, which is always depicted as a bird, the numbering of the Bamboo and Circles suits is shown on Mah Jongg tiles by a pattern of the number of bamboos or circles, similar to Western cards. Wan suits show the number by the appropriate Chinese numeral written in black and the character for 'ten thousand' below it in red. In the present set of Mah Jongg divination cards, the red character is the name of the suit, with the divinatory name of the card given beneath it in black. The name of this character appears in translation at the foot of the card itself.

The Honours Cards

The seven Honours cards consist of the four directions (usually known as the 'Winds' by western Mah Jongg players), and what are loosely, and incorrectly, called the three 'Dragons': Green, Red and White.

The cards for the four directions – East, South, West and North – are marked in black with the appropriate Chinese character. East ranks the first, and North the last, of the four directions.

The card marked with a green Chinese character means 'Commence' and the one with the red character 'Centre'. The White card is meant to be blank, but is shown with a panel, and can therefore be distinguished from the three blank spare cards supplied with the pack.

The Eight Guardians

The emblems portraying the eight Guardians vary considerably from one Mah Jongg set to another, and the cards are sometimes marked Spring, Summer, Autumn and Winter. There are two cards to represent each season, one usually depicting a seasonal flower or plant, and the other an appropriate occupation. In this set of cards, the most usual traditional forms have been retained: Plum Blossom, Orchid, Chrysanthemum and Bamboo for the flowers; and Fisherman, Woodcutter, Farmer and Scholar for the occupations.

Numbering of the Cards

The Mah Jongg Oracle cards presented here have been given identifying numbers to make it easier to find the appropriate reference in this handbook.

The twenty-seven suit cards are numbered from 1 (for 1 Bamboo), through 10 to 18 for the Circles suit, and up to 27 for the 9 Wan card. The numbering continues with the Honours cards in this order: East, South, West and North are cards 28–31; Commence, 32; Centre, 33; and White, 34. Finally, the eight Guardians follow the White card, from Plum Blossom, 35, to Scholar, 42. These numbers are printed at the bottom of the panel in red. They should not be confused with the suit numbers which are printed at the top of the panel in black.

How to Set Out the Cards for a Reading

The diviner, who interprets the oracle, and the querent, for whom the oracle is being read, need to sit at a table of suitable size: a space of about half a metre (18in or so) in diameter is needed for comfortable working. The Chinese, when it is practicable, prefer to arrange the placing of the table so that it is oriented North and South, with the diviner and querent facing each other East and West. They also dislike a situation where doors or posts are in direct line with the table as this is not regarded as being sym-

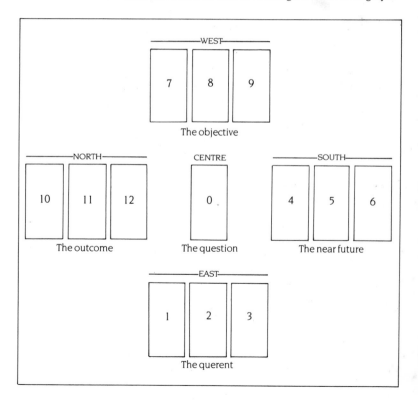

WEST

7 8 9

The objective

NORTH

10 11 12

The outcome

CENTRE

0

The question

SOUTH

4 5 6

The near future

EAST

1 2 3

The querent

pathetic to the oracle. Ideally, the querent should sit in the position left of South, in what is called the 'East' position, but what is geographically West, since the Earth is a mirror image of the Heavens.

The places being taken, all the Mah Jongg cards (except the three spare blank ones) are spread face down at random over the table.

The querent, using both hands, shuffles the Mah Jongg cards until satisfied.

The diviner (the person who is going to 'read' the Mah Jongg cards) should ask the querent whether there is a specific question for which an answer is sought, or whether a general reading is required.

If there is a specific question, this may be declared or not, as the querent wishes.

The querent then pushes the Mah Jongg cards to the edge of the working area until the whole of the central area is cleared.

Next, the querent draws thirteen Mah Jongg cards, still face down, into the central space, so making an 'island' of thirteen cards within a 'lake'.

These thirteen cards are reshuffled, still face down. The querent then 'rejects' three of the thirteen Mah Jongg cards by pushing them away, towards the West sector of the table – but still keeping them separate from the rest of the cards round the edge of the lake.

Similarly, three of the central thirteen Mah Jongg cards are then drawn towards the querent. Three others are pushed to the North, and another three to the South, leaving one card in the Centre.

The querent then carefully arranges the thirteen cards into four groups of three, according to the pattern shown in the diagram.

The cards are now ready to be interpreted, and the diviner may then take the East position.

The Centre card is numbered 0.

The other four groups of cards are counted left to right, moving from group to group in an anti-clockwise direction, starting at the near left.

The two outside cards of the East group represent one's surface personality, and the inner card the hidden self. Similarly, the two outside cards of the West group represent problems and obstacles, and the inner card the solution. For this reason, the outside cards of the East and West groups are turned over before the inner, so that the order of turning the cards over is as follows:

0, 1–3–2, 4–5–6, 7–9–8, 10–11–12

Note that the cards are not turned over all at once, but only as they are being read.

Inverted cards have no special significance, so that if a card is inverted when turned over, it need merely be replaced in its correct position.

If a Guardian card is turned over, then the querent selects another card from the edge of the lake, and the diviner replaces the Guardian card with the new card, positioning the Guardian card just above it.

Reading the Mah Jongg Cards

The diviner first picks up the Centre card. This represents the point of focus of the reading, and what is central to the present problems.

The diviner then picks up the card in position 1 in the East sector, then the card in position 3. These reveal the querent's exterior personality, and factors which dominate the present situation.

The card in position 2 in the East sector is then picked up. This reveals the querent's inner, unspoken wishes.

The diviner then reads the cards in the South sector, taking each one in turn before turning up the next. These cards, representing the near future, refer particularly to events which are already taking place, or being considered.

The cards in the West represent obstacles and objectives, and their solution. The first obstacle is revealed by the card in position 7 of the West sector; other factors are shown by the card in position 9; while the card in position 8 is the one indicating the way by which the obstacles can be overcome.

Then the diviner turns to the North sector. These cards represent the eventual outcome of the present, or future developments. Cards 10 and 11 may warn of difficulties, or continue to unravel the train of events revealed by previous cards. The card in position 12 represents the final outcome of events.

The outstanding feature of the Mah Jongg oracle is its use of four identical packs of cards. This frequently results in the same card appearing in more than one place in the reading, so enabling the diviner to trace the recurrence of important events as the thread of fate is unravelled. For example, the Centre card refers to the querent's question; if the same card reappears it is possible to judge the circumstances by the cards associated with it – and even the timescale of events from the card's position.

As the four directions are associated with the four seasons, it follows that each card represents a month in the year. As the Chinese New Year is traditionally the day to have one's future told, the cards in the East would represent the Spring, those in the South the Summer, the West the Autumn, and the North the Winter. If, however, Mah Jongg cards are being read at any other time of the year, the cards' positions may be understood to refer to the early months of the coming year, with the final card (twelfth position) revealing events a year hence.

If interpreting the cards for another person, it is not good practice to give the querent advice which cannot be acted upon. It is alien to the nature of the true Chinese philosopher to give fatalistic news. The soothsayers may forewarn of danger, but only so that its effects may be forestalled.

In the following card summaries, if a
card is not mentioned in a particular
position then it does not have an
especially significant meaning.

THE
CARDS

紙
牌

Chu

THE BAMBOO CARDS

The Bamboo cards are the first of the three suits. It is important that they are not confused with the single Guardian card (no. 38) also called Bamboo.

In traditional ivory Mah Jongg sets, because the 1 Bamboo tile is the first of all the tiles – the 'ace' as it were – it is distinguished from all the others by being the only pictorial suit tile (depicting a long-tailed bird), while all the other tiles merely indicate the number of the suit by being marked with the appropriate number of bamboo stalks. These are mostly engraved in green – the colour associated in Chinese philosophy with the element Wood, symbolizing creativity and life.

The bamboo is a wonderfully useful plant and the variety of purposes it serves is virtually limitless. Its leaves and shoots are used for food, but it is the extraordinary utility of the stems which is so remarkable. It is used for sewing needles, writing implements, cooking utensils, vessels, ornaments, bric-a-brac, storage boxes, furniture, houses and boats, while its lightness and strength mean that in Southeast Asia it is still preferred to steel scaffolding, even for supporting the tallest high-rise buildings. Thus the bamboo serves to illustrate the virtues of strength, uprightness, integrity and service.

Interpreting the Bamboo Cards

The nine Bamboo cards are probably the most human of the three suits, and generally indicate refinement and tranquillity, emphasizing inner happiness, family relationships and health rather than material gains. Taken together they are less concerned with fame and fortune than the improvement of the whole person, both mentally and physically.

Those who persevere will find eventual satisfaction: 'the opening of a flower cannot be hurried'. There is continuing development, communication, travel – especially over water – and eventual contentment. The steadfast Bamboos warn against acting on impulse, taking snap decisions, reversals or changes in policy, and impetuous action.

Bamboo, being an emblem of the Scholar, is a fortunate sign for those entering for examinations.

Patience and understanding are the key items in the advice given by the Bamboo cards. The Willow (9 Bamboo) teaches that flexibility is strength; consequently, in matters regarding difficult personal relationships, a noticeably large proportion of Bamboo cards would suggest that the present troublesome phase is a temporary one which will improve with time. More positively, the Duck (2 Bamboo) reveals the advantages of a steady partnership built through mutual trust – the ideal response to one asking about marriage, or even a business partnership.

Those who enquire about health will usually find that the response given by a Bamboo card is favourable; the Carp (4 Bamboo) and the Tortoise (7 Bamboo) are both symbols of longevity, while the Toad (3 Bamboo) represents healing.

On the other hand, those anxious to find quick successes and sudden wealth are likely to be disappointed by responses from the Bamboo cards, which generally indicate slow but steady progress.

To questions regarding travel, Bamboo cards may be seen to be favourable; a large proportion of Bamboo cards will indicate frequent journeys; 6 Bamboo (Water) reveals travel by or over water.

I Bamboo PEACOCK   K'ung 孔

I

Success
A Mature Lady

Being the first card, I Bamboo signifies success; but this brings pride, which may lead to vanity. The Peacock is the emblem of beauty, and represents a lady, in the prime of her life, gazing in a mirror. For the Chinese, the mirror is the symbol of the cosmos; the lady may be admiring her own reflection, or she may herself be reflecting on her own mortality. The mirror frequently indicates a change of direction in life.

CENTRE CARD The first of the Mah Jongg cards indicates success, but also hints at the need for caution. It was described to me by a venerable Chinese astrologer as being 'lucky, but not so lucky'. As an answer to most questions, the response is success at first, but be prepared for setbacks later – this is only the beginning of a new series of events. It warns against waste, selfishness and any rash expenditure.

The card often signifies an older woman. If the querent is a mature lady, it may refer to her; otherwise it may indicate concern for an elder relative, the elder of two sisters, or in the case of a romantic triangle, the elder lady.

POSITIVE ASPECTS Its appearance in the East in the **third** position shows quiet confidence; in the **second** position, selflessness and devotion to duty. In matters of romance, it signifies an elder lady, and the associated cards must be examined to see the context.

In the West, in the **eighth** (middle) position, it signifies: 'Heed the advice of the older woman'.

NEGATIVE ASPECTS The Peacock is often unfavourably placed in the **first** position (East), when it is an indication of self-esteem, and overbearing self-confidence which may lead to resentment.

In the West, in the **seventh** and **ninth** positions, and North, in the **eleventh** position, the courtesan in contemplation suggests that after the prime of life there is but descent to follow. It urges that one must be prepared for change; that the vanities of former days are past and that it is folly to live in hopes and expectations.

See Readings:
Cases 9, 10, 11
and 12

2 Bamboo DUCK

Ya 鴨

The Chinese believe that a pair of ducks remain together for life – so the symbolism of the Duck is an enduring partnership. It is the ideal response for anyone enquiring about their romantic prospects, whereas in questions of business it represents a firm partnership. The significance of the Duck will be enhanced if the cards East (representing the querent) and West (the partner) also appear.

CENTRE CARD As the Centre card, the Duck refers to a partnership. If the querent is already in a happy partnership, then in the remainder of the spread any card whose meaning is in doubt will refer to matters concerning that relationship (or business partnership, if the context or question suggests it).

Where there is no present partnership, it will suggest that one is imminent, so that for questions regarding marriage, it can be taken as a definite, positive reply.

When there has been a question regarding the health of a person, the Duck shows that care from another person is needed, suggesting nursing and convalescence.

POSITIVE ASPECTS The Duck is virtually always positive in what it has to reveal. In the East, in any position, it represents a caring personality; combined with the Toad (3 Bamboo) it would suggest someone greatly interested in the nursing and medical professions. In the *second* position it suggests that here is someone who is anxious about another person, or someone who would like to do more for other people.

In the South, there is a sign of happy times to be spent in the company of another, while in the North, the relationship appears to be more distant: perhaps the partnership sought will not be realized just yet, or possibly it refers to the marriage of a relative.

NEGATIVE ASPECTS In the West, the emphasis is shifted from the querent to the partner, especially in the *seventh* and *ninth* positions. Here it indicates problems arising from the partnership itself. The card in the *eighth* position should be inspected to see the solution to the problem.

2

Fidelity
Partnership

See Readings:
Cases 5, 6, 7
and 8

3 Bamboo TOAD Min 黽

Healing
Over-ambition

Where Westerners perceive the flecks on the Moon's surface to be the face of the 'Man in the Moon', the Chinese regard them as representing two creatures – the Hare and the Toad. The Hare is credited with knowledge of the recipe for the elixir of life; but the traditional three-legged Toad, while being another symbol of long life, is also a sign of the unattainable. This card is associated with medicine and healing, and though it represents both sickness and cure, when positively aspected it usually represents recovery from illness. In a bad position, however, depending on the context, it represents over-ambition.

CENTRE CARD Depending on the question, this card represents either health or ambition. If there was no specific question, the meaning of this card may not be clear until further cards have been revealed.

If the question is about health, the response shown by this card is that definite news is imminent, and that a time of anxiety will soon be over.

If the question concerns business, it may act as a warning against being involved in projects which are beyond present resources – financial or otherwise.

In questions of romance, it is advisable to see what other cards are revealed.

If the question concerns choice of career, the nursing and medical professions should be considered.

POSITIVE ASPECTS The most positive aspect of this card is the indication of recovery from illness, which is shown best in any South or the middle West (*eighth*) positions.

If the question is specifically about health, it also indicates recovery from sickness in the final (*twelfth*) position in the North sector.

In the East, it shows a person interested in medicine, nursing, or the caring professions.

See Readings:
Cases 4, 6
and 12

NEGATIVE ASPECTS In the West, *seventh* and *ninth* positions, it may indicate that plans have to be delayed through ill health; or else that present schemes are far too extravagant – the aims are at present too high.

4 Bamboo CARP

Li 狸

The Carp is a symbol of tranquillity and inner calm which leads to a long life. Passing its days slowly and sedately, the Carp inspires the sage to contemplation, freeing him from the besetting cares and pressures of modern life. The Carp's rich colours symbolize wealth and refinement.

This card, therefore, signifies peace and contentment, and freedom from anxiety. It reveals recovery from ill health, and long life. It indicates peace of mind – although it does not necessarily mean that troubles will be over; it may mean that one has come to terms with a difficult situation, so suggesting a compromise has been achieved. Associated with Water (6 Bamboo) it signifies wisdom, a long journey or continuing correspondence.

CENTRE CARD The answer to the question is beneficial. Although it may reveal that results will take longer than expected, prospects for the long term are extremely favourable.

In matters of health, it shows recovery. In questions of romance, it shows contentment rather than excitement. Financially, it advises guaranteed sound, long-term investments to speculative deals which are hoped to reap quick profits.

In matters of career, the Carp, representing knowledge and experience, suggests education.

If there is a question of travel, the indication is of a long single journey rather than frequent short ones.

POSITIVE ASPECTS The aspects shown by the Carp are almost all positive. It shows that financial dealings managed over a long period are at last coming to fruition, recovery from chronic illness, and satisfaction with the course of events.

In the South, it represents a long journey.

With the 1 card of the Bamboo, Circles or Wan suits, it indicates success in examinations.

NEGATIVE ASPECTS The only negative aspects shown by the Carp appear in the West, in the *seventh* and *ninth* positions, when it reveals that matters under consideration will take longer than anticipated.

4

CARP

Longevity
Peace

See Readings:
Cases 2, 9, 10, 11 *and* 12

5 Bamboo LOTUS   Lien 蓮

5

Enlightenment
A Child

The opening Lotus signifies new birth. The mystical symbolism is of a spiritual awakening, while on a more material level it indicates the birth of a child. Frequently, this card appears to those who have recently undergone an uplifting experience or, at the other extreme, endured some severe loss, financially or otherwise, resulting in the need to come to terms with the present and begin life anew. In such cases the new-born child represents the new direction which life can now take. Often, those who have received what may have been seen as an insurmountable set-back in their careers will find that life still has a great deal to offer, for people frequently have rich, untapped veins of resources which can now be called upon. There may be unfulfilled ambitions which now have the possibility of being realized. As the great Chinese philosopher Lao Tzu said, 'What may appear to be a calamity often gives rise to fortune.' Those who have suffered some personal loss will eventually come to terms with their situation. The opening flower may hint at the passing of grief.

CENTRE CARD For many enquirers, the Lotus brings the happiest of news, revealing a new birth within the family circle, especially if the question is of marriage or children. The Lotus as the Centre card may otherwise indicate an opportunity for a new life. If the querent is young, it can signify a new career, entering university, or leaving home.

When the question concerns finance, the response is that the present circumstances are favourable, and that the querent should perform everything with careful attention to laws and regulations.

POSITIVE ASPECTS The significance of the Lotus is always one of awakening and reassurance, new ideas and inner happiness. Contentment is signified.

See Readings:
Cases 2, 4, 5
and 8

NEGATIVE ASPECTS In the West, in the **seventh** and **ninth** positions, if the question refers to finance, it indicates that the querent should be on guard against fraud. In other cases, it warns that a child in danger will hinder the proposed course of action.

6 Bamboo WATER   Shui 水

6

Correspondence
Travel

The element Water signifies communication. This may be in the form of correspondence, or travel. More often it refers to frequent short journeys, such as regular commuting, rather than a lengthy single journey which is sometimes signified by the Carp (4 Bamboo) in certain positions. But if the Water card is repeated in different sectors of the spread (for example in the North and South sectors) it suggests the crossing of water. If Water appears with West, it indicates a visitor from a foreign country.

In any cases where the question concerns travel, correspondence or documentation, examine the adjoining cards to determine what other factors are liable to exert an influence on the situation.

CENTRE CARD The Water card gives a positive response to any question regarding travel. It is also linked with health and healing, so that a question regarding health receives a favourable reply. In other matters, Water as the Centre card indicates journeys; and frequent correspondence will be involved in order to achieve one's aims. With Heaven (9 Wan) or Tiger (8 Circles) it is a sign of international travel.

In choice of career, anything involving communication and dealings with people on a personal level will prove to be successful.

POSITIVE ASPECTS Water is one of the five elements of Chinese philosophy, associated with Winter, the direction North, and the Tortoise (7 Bamboo). The element Water produces Wood, and so reveals good fortune when it appears next to any cards regarded as belonging to the element Wood, such as the Willow (9 Bamboo), the Pine (2 Circles) or the Peach (6 Circles).

NEGATIVE ASPECTS The combination of the Chinese character for 'water' with that of 'fire' produces the character for 'calamity'. Water and Fire are not harmonious; a combination of Water with the Fire card (6 Wan) is an indication of danger. Examine the other cards in context to see the time factor involved, or the relevant circumstances. Caution is then advisable.

See Readings:
Cases 1, 3, 6
and 7

7 Bamboo TORTOISE Kuei

7

Thought
Progress

More often than not, the Tortoise card reveals that the querent is dissatisfied with the time taken for matters to be resolved. But there is far more to the symbolism of this card than the Tortoise's lethargic progress. This creature, living to a great age, has become the symbol of longevity – and since it manages to live so long, it must necessarily be experienced and wise. Another meaning of this card, therefore, is 'knowledge'.

The Tortoise is one of the four great Chinese astrological constellations, covering the northern part of the sky, and so is associated with the North, Winter, and Water – the element of the North. It is regarded as very fortunate if the Tortoise is found in the North sector of the board, next to the North card, or combined with Water (6 Bamboo).

CENTRE CARD If the Tortoise appears as the Centre card it indicates that although progress appears to be slow at the moment, nevertheless matters are gradually moving towards the desired end. By progressing slowly and carefully, much experience will be gained, which will put the querent in an advantageous position.

It gives a favourable reply to those entering for examinations, as it reveals the rewards of careful study. Those hoping to become involved in romantic relationships should be patient, while those suffering from chronic ill health are assured of eventual recovery.

POSITIVE ASPECTS The Tortoise shows that although matters at present may not appear to be moving in the right direction as fast as one would like, yet there will be success eventually.

The card reveals knowledge, experience, and patience, especially when combined with Water (6 Bamboo) or in the North sector.

See Readings:
Cases 1, 3, 4, 8,
11 *and* 12

NEGATIVE ASPECTS The negative aspects of this card are really subjective, showing dissatisfaction with slow progress. Patience is advised.

8 Bamboo MUSHROOM Chün 菌

In Chinese painting and sculpture, gods are often depicted holding a strange, whorled object which represents the magic fungus of immortality.

The intriguing nature of the Mushroom – a plant lacking flowers or leaves and yet resembling both – led to its being a symbol of the bizarre. This card, depicting the fungus of immortality, is therefore a sign of something out of the ordinary course of events. It is a sign of something remarkable, or curious, which causes people to wonder. This may be the result of an unexpected turn of events, or someone's behaviour suddenly becoming completely out of character. It often reveals a highly individual personality who is not afraid of being unconventional, perhaps making a bold decision to break with tradition.

In general terms, it may refer to some future occurrence, as yet unknown, but so extraordinary that the querent will be obliged to recall the oracle's foreknowledge of a remarkable event. Whether or not the event is favourable is immaterial, for the circumstances are entirely unexpected.

CENTRE CARD To a specific question, the response is that the solution lies where it is least expected. In financial matters, those who wish to speculate may hazard a risk on an unusual venture which is outside their normal field of operations. In romantic matters, it denotes a relationship which may cause offence in the family, perhaps because of a difference of ages, races or creeds. In matters of health, it suggests that unorthodox methods may be found beneficial to the patient. Those who ask about their career are likely to be drawn to a profession which has few practitioners.

POSITIVE ASPECTS Help is at hand where least expected; such is the advice given by the Mushroom when it appears in the middle (*eighth*) position of the West sector. In the South, it denotes an unusual, but happy, turn of events. In the East, it denotes a person with outstanding creative talents, perhaps with a highly individual style.

NEGATIVE ASPECTS In the West, *seventh* and *ninth* positions, it reveals danger from an unexpected source.

8

MUSHROOM

Immortality
Eccentricity

See Readings:
Cases 5, 6 and 8

9 Bamboo WILLOW   Liu 柳

Modesty
Compliance

When the cold winds of winter blow, the Willow tree bends before it, but once the winds have passed, it regains its posture, now clad in a fresh mantle of greenery. Thus the symbolism of the Willow is strength through flexibility. Diplomacy is the keynote. It may be best to comply with the wishes of the stronger; set-backs are only temporary, after which one is able to return, now revitalized.

The Willow also has healing powers – aspirin is actually a synthetic preparation of a natural medicament found in the bark of the Willow tree. This is perhaps the reason why the Willow is associated with mourning – it helps to soothe the troubled heart.

CENTRE CARD The Willow card symbolizes diplomacy. Problems are only of a temporary duration; let them pass. To specific questions, the response warns that this is not the time for making sudden moves; matters should be left to take their own course; later the querent will be in a better position to make a decision. In matters of health, the response is favourable.

POSITIVE ASPECTS Trees belong to the element Wood, which conforms with the East. When the Willow appears in the East sector, it reveals a person who is flexible and is able to change plans readily.

In the West, particularly in the *eighth* (middle) position, it usually signifies that the solution to one's problems lies in being ready to change or accepting modifications to plans.

In the North, it reveals that problems will only be temporary, and find their own solution.

NEGATIVE ASPECTS When the Willow appears in the West, in the *seventh* or *ninth* places, it indicates weakness. It suggests a refusal to face a confrontation, and too ready a willingness to give up one's rightful position. It signifies a need for greater firmness and resolution.

As the Willow is more suited to the North and East positions, it is sometimes unfavourably aspected in the South, where it often indicates carelessness and disregard for detail which may bring problems later.

See Readings:
Cases 2, 3, 8
and 9

28

Truth and sincerity generate the gift of prediction

Confucius

THE CIRCLES CARDS

銅

T'ung

The Circles cards are the original suit of the Mah Jongg tiles, the patterns of circles being the same as those found on Chinese dice and dominoes – the suits of Bamboo and Wan were added later. The similarity of the circles to coins leads to the belief that most of the Circles cards are concerned with money and business.

As the Chinese of old could plainly see, the Heavens are circular, as are the Sun and the Moon. The disc, therefore, became the sacred emblem of Heaven, and by contrast, the square was regarded as the symbol of the Earth (although Chinese scholars would not actually have believed it to be that shape). The combination of the circle and the square was used in ritual objects representing the union of Heaven and Earth, with the Emperor, representing mankind, at the Centre. The Heaven and Earth plate, a dial rotating on a square base, was perhaps the earliest astronomical instrument to be used by the Chinese.

The backs of mirrors, which were regarded as having an almost magical property, always bore a design which reflected the symbolism of the universe. The square and circle pattern was reversed; as the mirror itself was circular, the Earth was represented as a square at the centre. In the course of time, this cosmological pattern was used for Chinese coins, which used to be distinguished by having a square hole at the centre. It is probably believed that the reason for the hole was so that they could be strung together – indeed, there is a Chinese character which means coins strung together in this fashion – but this does not explain why the hole should be square, nor indeed, why the Chinese, unlike other nations, should have wanted to thread their coins on to a string in

the first place. The answer lies in the basic symbolism; the coins, being issued by the Emperor, symbolized the Emperor linking Heaven and Earth.

Interpreting the Circles Cards

The Circles cards are generally concerned with business and money. Even those cards which usually relate to personal relationships – 2 Circles, a young
man; 6 Circles, a girl; 8 Circles, an older man – often
relate to events concerning work or business.

If the majority of the cards in the spread are Circles, then business and finance is certainly going to
be foremost in importance for the time being. On the
other hand, if there are only one or two Circles cards
in the spread, take this as an indication that financial
matters are not going to be the querent's main concern over the next few months. This need not necessarily be a negative answer if the question was one of
finance; the position will remain steady with regards
to financial matters, but may improve in other ways,
such as perhaps by changing one's role, outlook, or
whatever.

In the case when the question concerned, say, romance, then the function of the three 'personality'
cards (2 Circles, 6 Circles, 8 Circles) will be important. If these are not present, but there is still a large
representation of Circles cards, it is worthwhile suggesting to the querent that priorities may not be in
the right order. Personal feelings are being allowed
to override common sense.

In matters of health, the presence of Circles cards
is nearly always beneficial, the Pine, Phoenix and
Dragon, in particular, indicating a speedy recovery.

I Circles PEARL

Chu 珠

IO

Refinement
Wealth

The first of the Circles cards is crowded with symbolism. Mah Jongg gamesters call this card 'the Moon from the Bottom of the Sea' – a delightful way to describe a pearl.

To the Chinese, pearls indicate refinement – but it is the refinement of the connoisseur, so suggesting luxury and wealth. In a fortunate position, it refers to the acquirement of honour; when unfavourably placed it indicates thoughtless extravagance.

CENTRE CARD As the Centre card it represents financial gain, the acquisition of honour, or success in examinations. If no particular question has been posed, it indicates that there is unexpected value in something whose worth has been underestimated.

In questions of romance, however, it often indicates a match based on financial considerations rather than love.

In matters of health, it shows an improving condition.

Generally, the Pearl suggests that one should attend to financial matters with care. With regards to oneself, although it indicates honour when favourable, it also reminds one to be honourable and circumspect.

POSITIVE ASPECTS In the *fourth, fifth* and *sixth* positions (South) it shows promotion, success in examinations, or financial reward arising from matters already known to the querent, although their value may not yet be entirely realized.

In the *tenth, eleventh* and *twelfth* positions it reveals similar successes, but not just yet.

In the *second* position, in the middle of the East sector, it is called Yin Teh, or Hidden Virtue.

NEGATIVE ASPECTS In the East, the Self, it warns against flattery. The circle represents a mirror into which the querent should look deeply. Guard against vanity and extravagance. In the West, with regards to financial matters, it reveals that it will be difficult to raise funds for the project; in matters of romance, a selfish and extravagant person. Whatever the question, if it is in the *eighth* position (the middle of the West) it means that further expenditure will be necessary.

See Readings:
Cases 2, 3, 6, 9
and 11

2 Circles PINE

Sung 松

The Pine tree's firmness and strength suggest a young man; it may mean a lover, a younger brother, or son, depending on the context of the question. If the querent is asking about one of two men – as, for example, of rival suitors – it refers to the younger, or more specifically, the gentler or more dependable of the two. Not only does the Pine's ability to weather the severest storms indicate a resolute person, it also suggests someone skilled in writing, or drawing (as distinct from painting). This is because the wood of the Pine makes the finest charcoal, and its soot the finest ink. Thus here we have someone who uses diplomacy against violence – the pen being mightier than the sword.

CENTRE CARD At the Centre, the Pine shows determination and success in the face of opposition. In matters of the heart, as explained above, the Pine reveals the gentle giant. To a question about health, it shows strength, and recovery after a chronic illness through patient determination.

POSITIVE ASPECTS The Pine is nearly always favourable, showing resolute perseverance and enabling one to complete a task despite whatever obstacles may lie in one's pathway. Although there may be problems, eventually these will be overcome. In the North, it shows inner courage and moral support in times of difficulty.

NEGATIVE ASPECTS The Pine has few negative aspects; these are almost always confined to the West sector of the spread, in the *seventh* and *ninth* positions, when it indicates troubles from a younger male person. Its interpretation will depend on the age of the querent, and the nature of any question posed. If the querent is a man, it sometimes reveals a younger rival, either in romance or business. For a woman, it can mean the threat to a relationship with a man younger than herself; for a mature lady it can indicate problems with a son. If the querent has not asked a specific question, and the identity of the person indicated by the Pine is in doubt, refer to the card at the Centre of the spread for further guidance.

II

Strength
A *Young Man*

See Readings:
Cases 7, 9
and 10

3 Circles PHOENIX

Feng 鳳

PHOENIX

Joy
Splendour

The Phoenix of Chinese legend is said to appear only in the reign of a benign Emperor, when the Earth and Heaven are in Harmony; it therefore signifies happiness.

It is the symbol of the Red Bird of Summer, one of the four great Chinese astrological constellations, and the most appropriate place for it to be found is therefore in the South, when it signifies a joyous event.

CENTRE CARD The Phoenix at the Centre is a sign that all is in harmony, and that all things are going to plan. In response to a question, the reply will be a positive sign of assurance (that is to say, if the question is framed in a negative or pessimistic way, the response is favourable).

To specific questions, with regards to health, there is recovery. If there is a question regarding marriage, it assures a happy match; if the couple are already married, the birth of a child. Those who enquire about financial matters are certain of success; those who wish to gain office may be confident of promotion.

POSITIVE ASPECTS Wherever it appears, the Phoenix is undoubtedly a sign of happiness and pleasure – though it is important to remember that the two are not always the same. Its positive qualities are those which bring inner joy and contentment. As it represents the Bird of Summer, it is a sign of great fortune when this card is taken to replace one of the Summer Guardian cards. As Summer is the season appropriate to the South, it signifies a joyous event whenever it appears next to the South card.

NEGATIVE ASPECTS The negative quality of the Phoenix is pleasure rather than happiness. In the West, *seventh* and *ninth* positions, the 'joy' is in an unfavoured place, revealing that time and money spent on transient pleasures prevents the ultimate goal from being reached. This may be a warning to the querent; on the other hand it may refer to some specific aspect of the problem which prevents the objective being attained. It signifies that priorities are wrong; in general, it is a sign that greater attention should be given to more serious matters.

See Readings:
Cases 5, 6, 10,
11 and 12

4 Circles JADE

Yü 玉

13

JADE

Worth
Perseverance

In China, Jade is prized above gold. But when Jade is taken from the ground, it is a lifeless piece of dull rock. It only acquires value when time, work and skill have transformed the raw stone into an object worthy of admiration by an Emperor. More than that, Jade does not rust, fade or decay – its treasure is there for all time. Jade, therefore, represents hard work, but work to a worthy end. It represents lasting values, long-abiding friendships, long life, and a sense of justice.

CENTRE CARD Its appearance at the Centre may have more than one possible interpretation depending on the context, but in brief it says that nothing has been in vain, and that one's hard work will bring lasting reward.

To those who find life's problems difficult to bear, or who are beset with a thousand troubles, it urges perseverance, for there will eventually be recognition.

To those whose personal attachments are going through a difficult phase, it serves to remind them that the ties which are the hardest to tie are the hardest to break.

Those with financial queries are asked to persevere even further; the rewards may not yet be in sight, but will repay handsomely those who have the patience, and nerve, to wait. In matters of health, it may be necessary to bear the present situation with fortitude, but that matters will eventually ease.

POSITIVE ASPECTS The Jade card brings great rewards for those who are unafraid of hard work. In the East, it reveals someone with high personal values; if in the *second* position, it shows someone who may be inwardly hurt by the rash behaviour of close friends and relatives, but who nevertheless would not presume to interfere in another's private affairs.

NEGATIVE ASPECTS This card would only be interpreted as a negative card by the idle, as it shows that the obstacles to inner happiness are caused by one's own failure to face up to the realities of life and work. Those who work harder than average seldom have time to consider the matter.

See Readings:
Cases 1, 2, 4, 6,
and 11

5 Circles DRAGON   Lung 龍

Luck
Fortune

The Dragon is the symbol of luck and fortune, and the insignia of imperial rank. It represents sudden and unexpected fortune, rather than the rewards of hard work, and is therefore associated with gamblers and gaming. In a fortunate position it signifies a stroke of good luck, but when badly aspected means money wasted either through gambling or risky ventures.

CENTRE CARD 5 Circles, the fourteenth of the twenty-seven suit cards, is the middle suit card, so it is particularly appropriate when this card turns up at the Centre of a spread. Even the pattern of the 'dots' on the card shows the layout of the five points, North, East, South, West and Centre. If no specific question has been given, its appearance in the Centre can be taken to mean unexpected good fortune, and the querent may expect a win in a lottery, or perhaps regain a forgotten debt.

As a reply to a question, the answer is extremely fortunate, bringing happiness and augmentation of rank.

POSITIVE ASPECTS In the *second* position (the middle card of the East sector) it sometimes signifies that rashness is tempered by caution (the 'Dragon' trying to get out), but it can also signify that a creative urge has not been allowed to express itself.

It shows the happy outcome of current events in the *fourth* and *fifth* positions in the South, with planned extravagance (as for a holiday or celebration) in the *sixth*.

In the *eighth* position (the middle card of the West sector) it means a fortunate outcome to a difficult situation, but that money must be spent in the process.

In the final (*twelfth*) position it indicates change, the possibility of travel, and a fortunate result.

See Readings:
Cases 2, 3, 10
and 11

NEGATIVE ASPECTS The appearance of the Dragon as one of the East or Self cards indicates rashness. It often reveals a highly extrovert personality with fashion flair, but a distinct lack of business sense. It is not good for the Dragon to appear in the *seventh* or *ninth* positions where it suggests malice, gossip, extravagance and waste.

6 Circles PEACH

T'ao 桃

The velvety texture of the Peach, its softness and its fragrance have been used by many different cultures to express the qualities of feminine beauty. The appearance of 6 Circles in a spread generally denotes the influence, appearance, or interference of a young girl.

Where the querent is a young man, the Peach most often represents his loved one. If the querent is a young girl and, because of the disposition of the other cards, the 6 Circles is not thought to represent the querent herself, the Peach may mean a rival. In the case of older querents, the Peach often represents a daughter or younger sister.

Because ladies of the Emperor's court led an idle and pampered life, by extension the Peach has come to mean extravagance and indolence. Additionally, when appearing in the *first* position, it shows interest in the creative arts, and matters of feminine interest.

CENTRE CARD In answer to a specific question, the answer is 'A young girl'. If there is no specific question, then a girl will be the focus of the querent's attention. It is sometimes a warning against self-indulgence.

POSITIVE ASPECTS The transitory nature of the Peach means that it is important for this card to appear in strong positions such as the *first* and last (*twelfth*). In either of these cases, 6 Circles indicates a fruitful romantic relationship. In the *eighth* position (middle of the West sector) the Peach indicates that the solutions to the problem will be found through a young girl. Where there is a specific question, not concerned with romance, this reply often means that a young female will be able to offer advice and assistance.

NEGATIVE ASPECTS In the South, *fourth*, *fifth* and *sixth* positions, there is a tendency to overspend.

In the West, in the *seventh* and *ninth* positions, there are quarrels, jealousy and infidelity. A young woman stands in the way of success

In the North, *tenth* and *eleventh* positions, there is need to reconsider present actions. In matters of business, there is great rivalry and underhand dealing.

*Feminine Beauty
Romance*

*See Readings:
Cases* 1, 7, 8, 10
and 11

7 Circles INSECT

Ch'ung 蟲

16

Industry
Skill

The Insect here symbolizes industriousness – the silk-worm spinning its thread, the ant building its city, the bees gathering in their food, even the cheerful cricket.

The Insect card is the counterpart of Jade (4 Circles). Whereas Jade represents sustained effort bringing lasting reward, the Insect card reveals bustling activity over a short period, perhaps for no eventual purpose, but sometimes for some temporary achievement.

The frailty of the Insect also symbolizes weakness; it may therefore indicate that a situation is not as weighty as imagined. The character 'insect', together with that for 'water' form the combination meaning Rainbow, again suggesting something transient – a nine-day wonder.

CENTRE CARD At the Centre, the Insect suggests that the querent is going to be involved in a great deal of unexpected activity, encroaching heavily on spare time. To a question regarding finance, it is not a particularly welcome sign, suggesting that profits will only be small for a great deal of effort. In romantic matters, however, the sign is often a good one, as the hectic activity may well be the preparations for a wedding.

POSITIVE ASPECTS Positively, the Insect card represents those activities which involve a great deal of concentrated effort over sudden bursts of time – particularly by a team of people with the same objective. Those who are involved in the performing arts will be familiar with the tension and involvement suggested by this card, as will those people dealing with the emergency services. Its position has very little effect on the meaning, though it is preferable for the card to appear in the South. The important points to note are the cards which are associated with it and, to a great extent, the context of the question.

See Readings:
Cases 1, 2, 7, 9,
10 *and* 11

NEGATIVE ASPECTS In the West, *seventh* and *ninth* positions, or the North, it warns of incursions into one's time and finances. In the East, where it represents the questioner, it suggests someone who may commence one job before another has been finished.

8 Circles TIGER

Hu 虎

The Tiger card is the most masculine of all the cards. It symbolizes authority and bravery, but also aggression. It represents an officer, or person in uniform, and as such often represents one's superiors, authority, the police, and faceless bureaucrats. It may also reveal the father, other senior male relatives, or the elder of two boys. Sometimes, if the questioner is male, and enquiring about personal relationships, depending on the context or type of question, it may represent the questioner, or an older rival. For a female enquiring about relationships, it signifies the more physically dominant of two suitors – the younger man being represented by the Pine (2 Circles).

The White Tiger is the constellation of Autumn, and it is particularly auspicious if the Tiger replaces one of the Autumn Guardians, or appears next to its associated direction, West.

CENTRE CARD The interpretation of the Tiger as the Centre card depends a great deal on the type of question posed; the direct answer is 'the older man'. If the querent has asked for a general reading, and 'older man' seems to have no immediate relevance, it is advisable to wait until more of the spread has been revealed, in which case any further doubtful cards can be referred to the Tiger at the Centre.

In matters of romance, its signification as the older suitor should be clear. In other cases it may also suggest that the querent has a rival.

In matters of finance and health, the card shows the need to deal with someone of higher authority.

POSITIVE ASPECTS The card represents strength, and help from someone in authority, especially in the *eighth* position (middle card of the West sector). It is favourable when it appears next to its associated direction, West. In the *second* position it reveals strength of character.

NEGATIVE ASPECTS In the East, it may represent an aggressive attitude. In the West (*seventh* and *ninth* positions) and the North it often indicates conflict with authority. This is particularly marked when it appears with the Sword (2 Wan).

Authority
An Officer

See Readings:
Cases 2, 3
and 11

9 Circles UNICORN Ch'i 麒

Foresight
Honesty

The Unicorn of Chinese mythology – one of the signs of the reign of a good Emperor – was regarded as having the power to see into the future, a talent which was passed on to those mortals who gazed into pools of water by the light of its burning horn. Accordingly, the significance of the Unicorn card is the ability to foresee events. This sometimes means the gift of clairvoyance, but more usually it merely indicates a natural prudence which enables some people to keep always one step ahead of their rivals. Such people have an innate ability to judge character with uncanny accuracy – to 'see through' people – although this is a trait that may not always be welcome.

CENTRE CARD The Unicorn at the Centre is nearly always a fortunate sign, and may be taken as a favourable response to most enquiries.

If there is no specific question, it signifies good news. If the question is financial, the Unicorn shows foresight, and the availability of privileged or inside information. To questions regarding health, it indicates recovery. In romantic affairs, however, it suggests a need to look beyond the present situation.

POSITIVE ASPECTS As the Unicorn is the sign of the reign of a good Emperor, the appearance of the Unicorn card in the South shows that matters are moving towards a fortunate conclusion. It indicates revelation and new ideas which should be acted on quickly.

A particularly interesting combination occurs when the Unicorn card appears together with the White card. This is a sign of someone looking into the future, and as such often denotes a person who has clairvoyant powers. This is also the case when the Unicorn card appears in the East, though in the *second* position it suggests that these powers are yet latent, or not being used to the full.

See Readings:
Cases 2, 4, 10
and 12

NEGATIVE ASPECTS An urgent need to look ahead, and to examine the future implications of present affairs, is shown when the Unicorn card appears in the West and North sectors of the spread.

Whether a nation or a family,
if it is about to flourish,
there will be fortunate signs,
and when it is about to perish,
there will be evil omens

Confucius

THE WAN CARDS

萬

Wan

The third and final suit of cards is usually known as the 'Character' suit by Western Mah Jongg players, since the ivory tiles are engraved with the Chinese numeral, and the character Wan, meaning 'ten thousand'. For simplicity's sake, the suit is referred to throughout this book by its Chinese name. Although Wan literally means 'ten thousand' the word is frequently used to mean any large number. For example, the Chinese literary expression 'ten thousand things' is used to mean the entire universe; 'ten thousand people' means everyone in the world, although 'ten thousand years' might mean eternity, or any long period of time.

The Chinese have three different characters for 'ten thousand'. The classical character (seen in this set of cards) is said to represent a scorpion, but as it needs twelve separate strokes to write it, accountants and mathematicians often prefer to use an abbreviated form which can be found in some Mah Jongg sets. The third form, the swastika, is only ever used in Buddhist religious texts, where the 'ten thousand things' symbolize the heart of the Buddha.

Unlike the Circles and Bamboo suits, which reveal considerable variety in the use of the colours red, black and green for engraving the tiles, the Wan suit cards are uniformly red and black.

Interpreting the Wan Cards

As a general rule, the Bamboo cards are identified with people and personal well-being, while the Circles cards signify wealth and material comforts. The Wan cards, however, represent abstract concepts, sometimes indicating the visionary, perfectionist, and theorist – someone for whom the realism of everyday life takes second place to the achievement of academic goals and the fulfilment of ideals.

But despite this general picture, two of the Wan suit cards are markedly concerned with the solid practicalities of living: 3 Wan (Earth), and 5 Wan (House), signifying land and the buildings which stand on it. The appearance of these two cards together is a marked indication of moving house or business, involving the purchase of property in its own ground.

Spreads which have a high proportion of the Wan suit cards often indicate highly complex situations – mathematical problems, chemical formulae, or legal entanglements. In this respect the Wan cards signify numbers, whereas the Bamboo suggest letters. It follows that if the querent were asking about career, the Wan suits suggest technology and science as distinct from the Bamboo cards which favour the humanities and literature, and the Circles cards which lean towards trade, banking, and merchandising.

For many everyday questions, if there is a high proportion of Wan suit cards in the spread, the querent would be disappointed. There is little here to suggest romance or warm personal relationships. Indeed, in many matters, the symbolism of the scorpion (the ancient form of the character for Wan) should be a warning to be on one's guard: a notable example is the 6 Wan card (Fire), which often suggests hidden danger. In matters of health, the 2 Wan (Sword) and 5 Wan (House) might suggest that surgery would be advisable. Again, in questions of personal relationships, the combination of 2 Wan (Sword) and 8 Wan (Knot) show the severing of a relationship. But 8 Wan and 9 Wan (Heaven) would be much more auspicious, showing a knot being tied with Heaven's blessing.

1 Wan ENTERING

Ju 入

A *Door*
A *Barrier*

The Chinese character for 'one' resembles the bar of a door, so the symbolism of 1 Wan is that of a barrier being lifted, or a door being opened, bringing new opportunities and perhaps a new life ahead. Only occasionally is the symbolism reversed, to mean that the barrier is an obstruction to one's aims. If the card replaces one of the Guardian cards, it signifies that although doors may appear to be closed at the moment, they will be opened eventually.

CENTRE CARD To a general question, the response can be interpreted as 'another chance'. If the question concerns a serious health problem, the symbol sometimes represents admission to hospital. In questions of romance, as it indicates a new life, it can be interpreted in the sense that a young couple will soon be beginning a new life together, but the interpretation may vary depending on the context of the question.

POSITIVE ASPECTS The Door reveals the new. The following card will give an indication of what is to be renewed. For example, when combined with 5 Wan (House), which represents a building, the symbolism is at once obvious: a door leading into a building, which might be a new home, place of employment, college, or university. If it appears with the Duck (2 Bamboo) it almost certainly indicates a marriage or a new partnership. With the Toad (3 Bamboo) it shows recovery from ill health. A move to a different location is shown by Entering followed by Earth (3 Wan). This card is in its best positions in the Centre, South, as the middle of the West sector (*eighth* position), or as the final (*twelfth*) card to be turned.

In the East it represents an innovator, someone who can bring new light and life to long-established projects.

See Readings:
Cases 2, 7, 10,
and 12

NEGATIVE ASPECTS In the West, *seventh* and *ninth* positions, and in the North, *tenth* and *eleventh* positions (but not as the final card) the Door appears to be firmly closed. Hopes and ambitions appear to be dashed; other people may not express their fullest confidence in the querent.

2 Wan SWORD

Chien 劍

The double-edged sword is the symbol of quandary and decision. Whereas 2 Bamboo (Duck) shows a partnership and the joining together of two people, 2 Wan signifies the opposite – severance. There can be no progress while there are still two; the situation will be a stalemate until some move is made. The Sword represents the element Metal; its appropriate colour is white, its season Autumn, and its direction West.

CENTRE CARD The Sword as the Centre card shows the querent faced with a dilemma. A crossroads has been reached; one road must be chosen or it will be impossible to travel further. Therefore, in order to progress, some sacrifice has to be made – the dilemma usually revolves on whether the sacrifice will be worth it. As an answer to a particular question, the Sword does not tell the querent which direction to take, only that a choice has to be made.

In other cases, the Sword may reveal the cutting away of ties, and release from contractual or other obligations.

POSITIVE ASPECTS The Sword represents the bonds being severed, and restrictions lifted, providing release at last.

There is a strong link between this card and the Knot (8 Wan). If the Knot is followed by the Sword, anywhere in the spread, it represents the severing of ties, and in this respect may signify resignation from employment, separation of a partnership, or emigration – any kind of weighty, irrevocable decision.

In the East, it represents diplomacy and fairness.

NEGATIVE ASPECTS Strictly speaking, the Sword has neither positive nor negative aspects, being a purely objective view of a situation. It directs the querent to be aware of problems, particularly the difficulties which have to be faced in trying to make two things out of one. Perhaps time is being wrongly allocated, or loyalties shared, or in some way attention is not being given to the things that are at the moment of greater importance.

As a negative personal characteristic, it represents hypocrisy and insincerity.

20

Balance
Decision

See Readings:
Cases 3, 4, 7, 8
and 12

3 Wan EARTH

Ti 地

Land
Estate

The Earth is one of the five elements of Chinese philosophy; it represents the fixed centre, and so does not belong to any season or compass direction. While this card may therefore symbolize the Earth element's attributes, usually it can be interpreted in the more literal sense of land, estate, wide open spaces, and the countryside.

The meaning of Earth as an element is stability. With the House (5 Wan) it presents a picture of a building standing in its own land. When it follows any card representing travel (such as Water, 6 Bamboo) it shows travel to another country over water.

CENTRE CARD Being associated with the Earth element, which belongs to the Centre, it is an extremely fortunate sign when this card appears at the Centre of the spread, when it means that one's ambitions regarding land or territory will be achieved. This may refer to the actual acquisition of land (as if one were buying a house), or thinking of moving to another area.

If the question did not concern land or territory (as, for example, a question about health or marriage prospects) then the fortunate placing of Earth at the Centre can be taken as a positive reply to the query. It may, however, contain the inherent suggestion that a move to another area would bring favourable results.

To questions of a financial nature, Earth represents real estate, stability, fixed assets. In matters of career, Earth suggests mining and civil engineering.

POSITIVE ASPECTS Its association with the Centre has already been mentioned; consequently it is also a fortunate sign when this card appears next to the Centre card, when its interpretation will be similar. Next to the Sword (2 Wan) it reveals wealth.

See Readings:
Cases 4, 6, 9
and 12

NEGATIVE ASPECTS The appearance of the Earth card next to Fire (6 Wan) cannot be regarded as fortunate, the two elements revealing aridity and famine. It is a sign that spending should be carefully monitored as a drain on resources is likely.

4 Wan LUTE

Ch'in 琴

The Lute represents the performing arts; it is a symbol of leisure, relaxation and a time for enjoyment after a day's or a lifetime's work. The literal significance of music is shown by the close proximity of Bamboo cards, particularly the Carp (4 Bamboo) or Water (6 Bamboo). With the Mushroom (8 Bamboo) there is an additional sense of the eccentric or 'fringe' performance. When the card is close to the industrious cards Jade (4 Circles) or the Insect (7 Circles) it symbolizes reward for honest toil.

CENTRE CARD The interpretation of the Lute at the Centre will depend very much on the nature of the question. In general terms, it indicates leisure and enjoyment, but when a specific question has been put to the oracle, the meaning is less easy to define. To take an example: if the querent were to ask, 'Which of the two should I marry?' and one of the choices is a musician, then there is no doubt as to the answer. But if the question posed were 'Is my love true?' the Lute suggests that this relationship is but a temporary dalliance.

To questions regarding health, it suggests recuperation through convalescence; in financial matters, gain through the leisure industries.

POSITIVE ASPECTS When in the South, the Lute reveals reward, relaxation, holidays, leisure and, more importantly, the favourable circumstances which make these activities possible. As the last card of all, it reveals reward for hard work, retirement, and the end of a difficult period.

NEGATIVE ASPECTS When in an unfavourable position the Lute reveals idleness and frivolity, and suggests that not enough time is being given to essentials. This is particularly the case when the Lute appears in the West, in the seventh and ninth positions. In the North, apart from the final card, it shows that future events are going to distract attention from the real work in hand. However, if the querent is a musician or performing artist, the presence of the Lute will be essentially favourable and will refer to career prospects.

22

LUTE

Music
Leisure

See Readings:
Cases 1, 6, 7, 11
and 12

5 Wan HOUSE   Fang 房

HOUSE

Institution
Home

The House represents any building; it may be the home, place of business, administrative offices, school or hospital. The essence of this card is that it signifies the tangible fabric of a building – the walls and roof – rather than its being the symbol of an organization or society. This is particularly the case when the House card appears in conjunction with Entering (1 Wan) (the symbol of a door), when it reveals the querent actually entering the building, or Earth (3 Wan), when it shows a building standing in its own grounds.

CENTRE CARD The House represents solidity and strength; when it appears at the Centre of a spread its interpretation depends on the question put to the oracle. If the reading is of a general nature only, then it reveals that the querent's home circumstances are being considered. To questions of marriage, it suggests that the essential matter of having somewhere to live is of prime importance. To questions regarding investments, or even career, it suggests that success lies in bricks and mortar. When the question concerns health, it may refer to the person concerned returning home, or going into hospital, depending on the way the question was posed – the remaining cards will clarify this.

If it appears with the West card (as distinct from being in the West sector) it may indicate a house or building which the querent does not occupy at present. This is also the case when it follows Water (6 Bamboo), as this suggests travelling to reach the building.

POSITIVE ASPECTS The House draws attention to a matter which might have been overlooked. Essentially, if it is in a fortunate position as in the South sector, or together with the South or another fortunate card, then matters concerning the home or business premises will be favourable.

See Readings:
Cases 7, 8, 10
and 11

NEGATIVE ASPECTS If the House appears in the West sector of the spread, *seventh* and *ninth* positions, it reveals that at the core of the problem is the querent being tied to a particular place – it may be the home or business premises. The card in the *eighth* position will reveal the course to take.

6 Wan FIRE

Huo 火

Fire is the third of the five elements of Chinese philosophy, representing the personal attributes of intelligence and inspiration. Yet of all the cards which comprise the Mah Jongg oracle, this is the card that gives the gravest warning of danger. It indicates the burning up of resources, mental, physical, and financial, and in combination with certain cards is a foreboding of accident to person or property.

CENTRE CARD At the Centre Fire is almost always a sign of danger; it is a direct indication that the querent must be on guard. In response to any query, it is a sign that there are other sides to the issue that have not been considered. Whatever the involvement, the querent should go carefully over all the aspects of the problem, to see what vital factor has been neglected.

However, if the question has been one regarding choice of career, it indicates the chemical or fuel industries. As it represents intelligence, it is also a favourable response to questions regarding educational prospects.

POSITIVE ASPECTS In the East, in the *first* and *third* positions, Fire is a sign of intelligence; in the *second* position, that the querent's talents are not being used to the full.

If a Guardian card has been replaced by the Fire card, it indicates that an accident or calamity will be averted.

NEGATIVE ASPECTS In the South, or with the South card, it indicates excess of Fire. For those who work with their brains, it indicates mental strain, tension, and nervous exhaustion. Fire next to any of the Bamboo cards is unfavourable; the Chinese characters for Fire and Water spell 'catastrophe' and the Water card (6 Bamboo) next to Fire indicates a disaster. If North is also close to the Fire–Water congruence, it reveals legal problems and criminal proceedings. If Fire is together with Earth (3 Wan) it shows the drying up of resources; if it follows the Dragon (5 Circles), it shows that there has been carelessness in the handling of finances, and former good fortune will be consumed – but if Fire precedes the Dragon the cards are to be interpreted separately.

24

Inspiration
Danger

See Readings:
Cases 4, 9
and 12

Hope
Literature

7 Wan SEVEN STARS   Tou 斗

Whereas Fire (6 Wan) represents intelligence, the Stars indicate imagination. The Seven Stars represented are the stars which form the familiar pattern of the Plough, part of the Great Bear of western astronomy. The ancient Chinese believed that this constellation was the seat of the gods, particularly the god of Literary Excellence. Consequently, this card may refer to writing, mathematics, or literature, particularly if it appears in conjunction with the Pine (2 Circles). With Water (6 Bamboo) it indicates journals, diaries, and accounts. In the East, the Stars indicate a literary person, frequently a dreamer rather than someone who can put ideas into action.

CENTRE CARD The Stars in the Centre position indicate the querent's present hopes and desires; in a general reading, the remaining cards unravel the course of events, relating to these ambitions.

When a specific question has been asked, the response shown by the Seven Stars is to ask the querent whether sufficient thought has been given to the practicalities of the problem; the ideas are there, but brilliant though they are, there seems to be a need for greater thoroughness in matters of detail. However, if the Stars, as the Centre card, replace a Guardian card, it will still be safe to proceed, though bearing this warning in mind.

POSITIVE ASPECTS Dreams and ambitions may be realized if the Stars are in a favourable position, perhaps preceding the Entering card (1 Wan), or next to Heaven (9 Wan) which is the realm of the stars. With the Centre (Red) card, it shows objectives are attained, while if Commence (Green) follows, it is a sign that the querent's ideas and suggestions should be acted on without delay. This is also the case when the Stars appear in the *eighth* position.

NEGATIVE ASPECTS Next to the Toad (3 Bamboo) or the Pearl (Moon, 1 Circles) the dreaming stars suggest someone yearning for the unattainable. Badly aspected, as in the West, in the *seventh* and *ninth* positions, it is a sign that present plans are not realistic, and ought to be revised.

See Readings:
Cases 3, 5 and 8

8 Wan KNOT

Chieh 結

This is perhaps the most enigmatic of all the Mah Jongg oracle cards, for it represents both the tying and the untying of a Knot. Perhaps more than any other card, the true meaning of the Knot can only be understood in the context of whatever question was presented to the oracle, and the cards which are to the side of the Knot.

If the Sword (2 Wan) is close by, then the meaning is at once apparent: a knot has to be severed. But with the Duck (2 Bamboo) which represents a partnership, the Knot is obviously being tied. The Knot is a sign of problems and anxieties. When it appears in the East, representing the querent, it reveals indecision. If it appears in the *first* or *third* positions, it shows other people get the impression that the querent is not sufficiently determined. If in the middle (*second*) position it shows inner fears and nagging doubts.

CENTRE CARD At the centre, the Knot indicates that the querent is faced with a quandary. If no specific question has been asked, then the circumstances imply the threat – or promise – of becoming involved in a situation which may require a heavy commitment, and the querent does not yet feel ready to take on such responsibility.

In the case of a specific question, the Knot returns to the querent, asking how much of the problem is due to a reluctance to tie or untie bonds. Very often, the answer lies in determining to what extent the querent is prepared to make sacrifices in order to achieve the desired ends.

In financial problems, it may signify funds which could be used if they were not already tied up elsewhere. In questions of health, it shows that the present situation is not yet resolved (decisions should be taken when the course of the illness becomes more apparent).

POSITIVE ASPECTS With the Duck (2 Bamboo), or the Commence (Green) card it shows a favourable partnership. With Jade (4 Circles) it indicates involvement in a beneficial long-term project.

NEGATIVE ASPECTS Any unfavourable aspects of the Knot (anxieties, commitments, ties) will depend on its context.

26

Tying
Untying

See Readings:
Cases 1, 3, 4, 5
and 10

9 Wan HEAVEN

T'ien 天

Fulfilment
Achievement

The Heaven card represents completion. But it does not mean an end, for when one cycle ends, another naturally begins. When the Heaven card appears next to that of the House (5 Wan), it represents the Temple; it only needs the Door (Entering, 1 Wan) to obtain the picture of someone entering the Temple to take part in a solemn celebration. If Heaven and Earth are next to each other, it signifies that when the events on Earth follow Heaven's laws everything is in order, and happiness and prosperity abound.

CENTRE CARD Heaven indicates that one of the stages in life has come to a conclusion, and another is about to begin. This message will be emphasized if the Commence (Green) card appears later in the spread.

POSITIVE ASPECTS The religious rites which are symbolized by this card represent birth, marriage and death. Birth will be shown by the 'young man' or 'young girl' cards (Pine, 2 Circles, and Peach, 6 Circles), marriage by the Duck (2 Bamboo) and death by the White card. But as this card can never have an unfavourable interpretation, its appearance in the latter combination refers to someone who has already passed away. Thus in such a case it may refer to the estate or effects of a deceased person, or it may be an exhortation to the partner left behind.

It is fortunate when any of the astrological symbols appear next to Heaven. Heaven is looking down favourably when it appears next to the Moon (Pearl, 1 Circles), the Stars (Seven Stars, 7 Wan), or the constellations of the Dragon (5 Circles), Bird (Phoenix, 3 Circles), Tiger (8 Circles), or Tortoise (7 Bamboo). In these cases, any negative aspects will be protected by the positive virtues of the Heaven card.

If Heaven replaces any of the Guardian cards, this must be regarded as extremely propitious, as it reveals one of the Heavenly Guardians bringing mystical powers to one's aid. Frequently, this refers to inexplicable circumstances which the querent has experienced.

See Readings:
Cases 1, 2, 7, 8
and 9

NEGATIVE ASPECTS As Heaven is perfection, this card can never have a negative interpretation.

By nature, people are all alike.
It is their behaviour which makes them different

Confucius

Sze

Fang

THE HONOURS CARDS

The three suits are complemented by seven independent Honours cards. Unlike western playing cards, where there are three 'court cards' for each suit, the Mah Jongg Honours cards do not belong to any particular suit.

Four of them are the directions East, South, West and North, often called the Four Winds. Western players usually call the remaining cards the Three Dragons: Green, Red, and White on account of the colours in which the tiles are engraved (or not, in the case of the White). With the exception of the White (or 'blank') card, the names of the Honours cards appear on them in Chinese characters.

Chinese philosophy dictates that to the four principal directions (East, South, West and North) must be added the Centre. Thus in the Mah Jongg the four direction cards are supplemented by the fifth cardinal point – the Centre. This is the pivot from which the others radiate, or in astrological terms, the Pole Star round which all the other stars make obeisance; thus the Centre is associated with the Emperor, at the very hub of the Middle Kingdom, as the Chinese call their country. In traditional Mah Jongg sets, the ivory tiles representing the four directions are engraved in black, while the Centre, *Chung*, is distinguished by being engraved in imperial red. The red Centre card is complemented by a green one bearing the Chinese character *Fa*, meaning 'commence'. It is perhaps no more than a coincidence that the colours employed for these two tiles should be accepted in the western world as the signals for 'stop' and 'go'.

Finally, the third of the three 'dragons' was formerly one of the plain, blank tiles kept as a spare. But as it has long been accepted as a piece in its own right, the 'blank' or White tile is usually distinguished from the spare tiles by having a border or frame engraved on it. Some Mah Jongg sets have the letters R, G and W engraved on these tiles (for Red, Green and White) which indicates that these sets were destined for the English-speaking world. However, sets from the turn of the century intended for non-Chinese use are marked with the letters C, F and P (for *Chung, Fa* and *Pai*) instead, so demonstrating that foreign players originally knew these pieces by their Chinese names, and not as the three dragons.

Interpreting the Honours Cards

The interpretation of the four directional Honours cards is essentially linked with the meanings of the symbolism of the seasons, and their respective elements – thus the South represents success, and prosperity; the North distress, and poverty. Nevertheless, it is considered harmonious for any of the four directions to appear in its appropriate quarter of the spread, while the unfavourable influences of the North are countered by those of the South, whether by South appearing in the North sector, or vice versa.

Of course, the directional pieces may also refer to an actual direction or location, if such is suggested by context. Nothing would be more appropriate as an answer to the question, 'In which direction should I travel?' than for one of the directional cards to appear as the response in the Centre. Of course, should the Centre appear, this would clearly indicate 'Stay put!'.

The *Fa, Chung* and *Pai* cards can always be regarded as favourable. In particular, nothing could be more auspicious than the Three Blessings, when *Chung*, the Centre, appears at the centre of the spread, *Fa* (Commence) in the first position, or White as the final card turned.

EAST

Tung 東

28

EAST

The Querent
The Present

The Chinese character for 'east' shows the sun rising behind the trees. In the game of Mah Jongg, the dealer sits in the East position; in the oracle, the East represents the querent, and the present situation. The East card indicates that at the time associated with the card's location, the querent will be involved in an incident which will prove to be of lasting importance. The East is associated with the Spring and the colour green; its astrological constellation is the Dragon (5 Circles) and its element Wood.

CENTRE CARD As the East represents the querent, the appearance of the East card at the Centre of the spread is a sign that something of personal importance is to be given careful consideration. If the oracle is being consulted on another's behalf, the East card directs the question back at the querent, suggesting that insufficient attention has been given to one's own involvement.

To a question regarding romance or marriage, the answer must lie with the querent; it is not for other people to make decisions. In business matters, more personal commitment may be necessary. If the question concerns the querent's own health, the East card suggests that there is still a lot which can be done by one's own efforts. Regarding choice of career, the connection between East and the creative element Wood suggests a wide choice of professions, all connected with life and growth.

POSITIVE ASPECTS When in a good position, and placed next to favourable cards, the East card represents personal success. The Dragon (5 Circles) brings short-term financial rewards. In the South or next to a South card it shows happiness. Next to the West card it indicates a partnership.

NEGATIVE ASPECTS As the East represents the Self, it is not considered to be favourable when the East card occurs in the East sector, in the *first* or *third* positions of the spread, because this means that too much attention is given to oneself. But if the East card occurs in the *second* position, then this indicates that the querent puts consideration for others before self-interest.

See Readings:
Cases 1, 2, 4
and 5

SOUTH

Nan 南

29

Success
Reward

The life-giving Sun occupies the realms of the South, symbolized by luxuriant vegetation. Because of this, for thousands of years Chinese Emperors took care to have their palaces built with the throne room facing south, so enabling the Emperor to look on his divine parent.

The South is therefore considered the most fortunate direction, and always indicates success. The appearance of the South card is therefore regarded as extremely propitious, since it promises a favourable outcome for any affair represented by the cards next to it.

It is associated with the Summer, the colour red, the astrological constellation of the Phoenix (3 Circles) and the element Fire.

CENTRE CARD The South card at the Centre indicates a favourable response. Matters will proceed as planned, and result in success. If the reading is a general one, it shows a stroke of good luck; the wish will be granted.

In matters of romance, the sun shines favourably on the relationship. In questions of business, the project may proceed with confidence. If health is a concern, a marked improvement in the condition can be expected shortly.

POSITIVE ASPECTS This card invariably spells success. In the East, it reveals a person of a sunny disposition; if it appears in the *second* place, however, it may be that the person wears a serious face, and is often a little afraid to let an inner, mischievous nature come to the fore. In the South, it reveals happiness and good fortune arising out of a current event. In the West, in the *eighth* position, it stresses the need for optimism, and a promise of future success. In the North, it is able to dispel the cold chill of a financial setback, and provide practical help when it is most needed.

NEGATIVE ASPECTS This very vital and positive card can only be interpreted negatively when it appears in the West sector (*seventh* and *ninth* positions) when it warns against the dangers of over-confidence. Light-heartedness and carefree living may take its toll; it is necessary to guard against leaner days.

See Readings:
Cases 5, 6, 7, 8
and 12

WEST

Hsi 西

30

WEST

The Objective
The Partner

The West represents the objective – that which the querent has to face. It may be a partner – in life, or in business – or it may represent obstacles.

Whenever the querent asks a question on behalf of another, the West will represent the other person.

The West's associated season is the Autumn, its colour white, its astrological constellation is the Tiger (8 Circles), and its element Metal.

CENTRE CARD In the Centre of the spread, the West either represents the partner, or the opposition. If no specific question has been asked, then the West usually represents another person, and it may be that the querent is subconsciously asking on someone else's behalf.

If the question is regarding marriage, or a relationship, then this is a fortunate sign. If there are problems concerning other people, then in this instance the West represents the opponent or rival. In questions regarding business, it suggests that the onus of responsibility belongs to the partner. In matters of health, it suggests that further opinion should be sought.

POSITIVE ASPECTS For anyone contemplating marriage or engagement, this is an excellent sign, as it represents the partner. The same is generally true of anyone thinking of entering a business with someone else, unless there are ominous signs which warn against the partnership.

The West represents the setting Sun, and retirement; it is a fortunate sign, therefore, when the West appears next to the Lute (4 Wan) for those who are about to retire, or are contemplating taking a holiday.

NEGATIVE ASPECTS When the West appears in the Western sector of the spread in the **seventh** and **ninth** positions, it represents strong opposition to the querent's plans; but if it occupies the middle (**eighth**) position then the querent should seek the answer elsewhere, perhaps by seeking the advice or assistance of a partner or friend.

In many cases the West adversely affects the meaning of any cards in association with it.

See Readings:
Cases 1, 3, 4, 6
and 10

NORTH

Pei 北

Distress
Poverty

The North, being the region never visited by the Sun, is regarded as an inauspicious direction, representing cold, famine, difficult times, privation and discomfort. Thus the North card indicates a cold wind, meaning a drain on resources, a period of unhappiness, worry, and conflict with authority. Sometimes it represents a person in authority — the senior employer, or legal representative.

The North is associated with Winter and the colour black; its astrological constellation is the Tortoise (7 Bamboo) and its element Water.

CENTRE CARD At the Centre, the North signifies a negative response. The planned course of action is defective; the expected help will not be forthcoming; promises will be broken. If a general reading is being given, the indication shows the need to be prepared against loss. If the question concerns romance, one must be prepared for disappointment. If there is financial concern, the prospects are not promising. However, if the enquiry concerns choice of career, the North indicates the military or civil uniformed occupations, and the legal profession.

POSITIVE ASPECTS If the North appears in its own sector, it is a sign of difficulties which had been foreseen. It may refer to a normal financial recess as, for example, might be expected with seasonal occupations. It may also refer to accidents or losses which had been insured against, and so can be regarded as a reminder to ensure that current policies and premiums are in order.

While North represents a person in authority, this can be beneficial when North is next to an appropriate card, such as Water (6 Bamboo), or the Tortoise (7 Bamboo).

NEGATIVE ASPECTS The North indicates disputes when it is close to the West or the Tiger (8 Circles), and financial loss when next to the Pearl (1 Circles) or the Peach (6 Circles). In the West sector, in the *seventh* and *ninth* positions, it reveals trouble with authority, but in the *eighth* position, it suggests that one must resolve one's disagreements, and follow the advice of someone higher in authority.

See Readings:
Cases 3, 8
and 11

COMMENCE Fa 發

32

Inaugurate
Proceed

Although the Chinese name of this card means 'to commence' it is usually called the 'Green Dragon' by western Mah Jongg players because in ivory sets the character Fa is invariably engraved in green ink. The Chinese character is a stylized representation of a bow being drawn, with an arrow ready to be fired. It is considered one of the Three Blessings when it appears in the *first* position in the spread, that is the card on the far left in the East sector, as this is the first card to be turned up after the Centre card. In this position it denotes a forthright and ambitious person, destined to achieve success.

CENTRE CARD This card gives the go ahead for any new enterprise. If there are doubts about embarking on new schemes, this card is a reassuring sign that one can proceed with confidence. Those who are unhappy about their romantic relationships are told to be bold and take the initiative. The querent who is considering a financial risk should avoid delaying a decision. Regarding health, this card expresses confidence in the patient's recovery.

POSITIVE ASPECTS This is an excellent sign for the inauguration of any new enterprise. If the time factor is in question, then the position of the card in the spread will give a hint as to the best time to act – the later the card appears in the spread, the later will be the most favourable moment.

If the Heaven card (9 Wan) appears it is best that this precedes the Fa card, since Heaven marks the end of one cycle and Fa the beginning of the next, showing that as one door closes, another is opened. In this respect, it is also extremely favourable if this card is followed by the Entering (1 Wan) card which represents the Door through which one passes to the next stage.

NEGATIVE ASPECTS It is preferable for this card not to be followed by Heaven (9 Wan) as this shows a distraction: a sudden new venture which is abruptly terminated, whether this be a financial dealing, romance, or whatever.

If the card appears in the *seventh* or *ninth* positions, it indicates the fear of taking a positive action.

See Readings:
Cases 4, 7 and 9

CENTRE

Chung 中

This card is known to western Mah Jongg players as the 'Red Dragon' since the Chinese character *Chung* meaning 'Centre' or 'Middle' is traditionally in red ink on the tiles of ivory Mah Jongg sets. This simple character clearly represents an arrow striking the centre of a target; it is the counterpart of the 'Commence' card, which shows the arrow about out to leave the bow.

The Centre is the fixed point of the five directions, associated with the element Earth, and the colour yellow. Its astrological constellation consists of the stars which rotate round the Pole Star, and is represented by the Seven Stars (7 Wan).

This card shows the achievement of objectives, success, fame, and the realizations of ambitions.

CENTRE CARD When the Centre card appears in the Centre of the spread, this is regarded as an extremely fortunate sign, and is one of the Three Blessings. In a general reading, it is interpreted as great fortune, a lucky chance, and great success. In matters of the heart, it shows a deep romantic involvement – the resemblance of this character to the traditional lover's symbol of a heart pierced by an arrow is clear enough. Those who enquire about financial matters will achieve riches; those who are sick will recover. In questions of career, farming, civil engineering and geophysics are highlighted.

POSITIVE ASPECTS This card reveals success and achievement. Because it is connected with the element Earth, it is doubly fortunate when it is next to the Earth card (3 Wan).

NEGATIVE ASPECTS In the East sector, which represents the querent's personal qualities, the Centre may indicate someone with markedly Earth-element characteristics (although these are not necessarily negative traits). In excess, these qualities give the impression of boorishness in one who prefers to be outspoken rather than diplomatic. In the *seventh* and *ninth* positions in the West sector, the negative quality of the Centre may manifest itself as over-ambition, and inflexibility.

33

色
中
33

CENTRE

Achievement
Success

See Readings:
Cases 3, 5, 7
and 9

WHITE

Pai 白

34

WHITE

The Unknown
The Departed

The White card, called the 'White Dragon' by western Mah Jongg players, was originally a spare blank one which eventually became accepted as a card in its own right. This card can be interpreted on two levels. Being blank, it represents the mysterious unknown, while the more prosaic interpretation is a white piece of paper waiting to be written on – the reply to a letter, or a contract about to be signed. Which of these two interpretations pertains depends very much on the overall circumstances, taking into account the type of querent, the nature of the question, and the associated cards in the spread.

The White card frequently appears more than once in readings given to those who are deeply interested in spiritual or religious matters, and is a sign of mystical involvement. To the Chinese, white is frequently associated with departed spirits. In cases where there has recently been a bereavement, this card can be interpreted as a sign of comfort. Associated cards which stress the spiritual side of White are the eight Guardian cards and Heaven (9 Wan).

The more commonplace interpretation of White is to be found when the question posed is of a more material nature, while the relevance of the associated cards should also be taken into account. The Earth card (3 Wan) is a clear direction that spiritual matters are not under consideration, while the Pine (2 Circles) represents the ink waiting to be put on the paper.

CENTRE CARD When White appears at the Centre, it should be interpreted in its mystic sense. The querent may have recently experienced a bereavement, or possibly has psychic gifts.

POSITIVE ASPECTS The White card, appearing in the last position of all (in the North, *twelfth* position) is one of the Three Blessings. It reveals a new and happier life waiting ahead.

In the East, it signifies an interest in the occult.

NEGATIVE ASPECTS In the West, *seventh* and *ninth* positions, it shows an irrational fear of the unknown, but may also represent difficulties caused by a document's invalidity.

See Readings:
Cases 1, 2, 5
and 12

The wise man is free from perplexity,
The bold man from fear,
and the virtuous man from anxiety

Confucius

仙

Hsien

THE EIGHT GUARDIANS

The eight Guardian cards form a completely separate pack of their own, and unlike all the other cards of Mah Jongg, the eight Guardians are not repeated. They comprise two sets of four cards, representing the four seasons – Spring, Summer, Autumn and Winter. One of the great attractions of antique hand-engraved Mah Jongg sets lies in the many different ways in which the four seasons are depicted; they are usually symbolized by flowers, or occupations appropriate to the particular season, but there are many fascinating variations to be found.

The reason for the curious division of the Mah Jongg cards into two distinctly different packs is due to the fact that the present-day version of the gambler's Mah Jongg is an amalgamation of two types of game; in one, the players score points according to the numbers marked on the pieces – as in dice, dominoes, or conventional playing cards. In the other type of game, the object is to collect sets of similar cards, the winner being the one who first compiles the required number of tricks. Traditionally, the first type of game is regarded as a man's pastime, and the other a woman's. Even to this day, on New Year's Eve, Japanese ladies play a game which uses forty-eight flower cards (four for each month of the year) and perhaps because of this, Japanese Mah Jongg sets often omit the eight Guardians.

The flowers usually chosen to represent the four seasons in Mah Jongg – Plum Blossom, Orchid, Chrysanthemum and Bamboo – are known as the 'Four Nobles' of Chinese painting, the pinnacles of artistic perfection. They were not only representative of the four seasons: each was an example of a different kind of plant, making its own particular contribution to the delight of the human senses.

The other four Guardians are represented by four occupations – Fisherman, Woodcutter, Farmer and Scholar – considered by the Chinese to be poor and humble callings, yet industrious, honest, and unfettered.

Together, the eight Guardian cards are representative of the Eight Guardians of Taoism – eight mortal beings who through their asceticism and pious works were transported to the celestial realms.

Interpreting the Eight Guardians

The role of the eight Guardian cards is rather different from the other Mah Jongg cards. They have no 'points' value, and when a Guardian card is turned up, another is chosen to take its place, although the Guardian card is retained. In Mah Jongg divination, when a Guardian card appears, the querent chooses another card, putting it on the spot previously occupied by the Guardian card, which is then placed just above it.

Guardian cards, instead of being read independently, are interpreted in the light of the associated card, whose message they influence and modify accordingly. In addition, they may also indicate the time factor involved in the matter under consideration, perhaps revealing the season when a particular occurrence may be expected.

The Guardians reveal help, advice, and guidance through difficult times. The replacement card indicates the type or source of some problem which is eventually alleviated. Because they always indicate help in times of difficulty, Guardian cards can always be regarded as having a 'positive' influence. However, they may reveal that a situation which appears to be beneficial may prove troublesome, albeit only temporarily.

PLUM BLOSSOM   Li 李

PLUM BLOSSOM

Love
Youth
Spring

After the starvation, cold and privations of Winter, vivid blossoms clothe the plum trees in a blaze of colour even before the leaves have budded. It is one of the first signs of Spring, itself the time of romantic love and awakening life. Thus the Plum Blossom symbolizes innocence and inexperience. For the young – and the young at heart – who are happily tied in romance, the Plum Blossom reflects happiness. It is the sign of renewed vitality, a new life, and all the fortune it brings.

The Plum Blossom Guardian card is in its most appropriate position in the East, or when near to an East card. Because the East also represents the querent, the Plum Blossom card refers back to the querent's personal situation, providing mental and physical protection, but guarding particularly against emotional stresses.

This is, therefore, a welcome card when there are inner anxieties, unexplained depression, problems which the querent is afraid to face, or an apparent sense of unwelcome personal obligation which is difficult to define. In such cases, the card taken to replace the Plum Blossom Guardian should be seen as the clue to the unravelling of those problems; once the situation is faced squarely, the nagging feelings of doubt and unease will be dismissed. This response will be doubly underlined if the card drawn to replace the Plum Blossom Guardian is the Knot (8 Wan), while the Sword (2 Wan) is a remonstration to cut oneself off from an involvement which is proving to be a wasteful drain on one's resources.

CENTRE CARD The Plum Blossom Guardian in the Centre position provides protection for all manner of things connected with love, life, emotions and inner happiness. When the question concerns these matters, this card shows a positive response. If the card drawn to replace the Guardian appears to give an adverse response, then the Plum Blossom Guardian shows protection through the difficult period. In matters which do not concern the querent personally – as, for example, in dealings with finance or estate – the response will be revealed in the card drawn to replace the Guardian.

See Readings:
Case 5

ORCHID

Lan 蘭

36

ORCHID

Refinement
Elegance
Summer

The Orchid is no common plant, and its pleasures are reserved for the privileged few. It indicates refinement, and is also a symbol of the rare and precious.

The essence of refinement is a continual process of improvement until absolute perfection is reached, and this quality is indicated when the card drawn to cover the Orchid is Jade (4 Circles). These cards then reveal that great honours are in store as the reward for continually striving to attain the highest standards.

The more material sense of precious treasure is revealed when the Orchid is replaced by the Pearl (1 Circles) or the Peach (6 Circles), when the Orchid indicates that something – or someone – of great value is being protected. The Orchid Guardian protects young girls, and if it appears in response to a question about a daughter or younger female relative, it serves to allay any anxieties regarding their welfare.

Being the flower representing the Summer season, it is appropriate for this card to appear in the South sector, or next to one of the South cards; in such a case it indicates future prosperity.

When it appears with a card said to be in an unfavourable position, it offers protection against the difficulties shown by the replacement card.

CENTRE CARD The Orchid Guardian, signifying the protection of something precious, is an extremely favourable sign in the Centre position when the question pertains to small valuable items such as jewellery, and shows recovery after loss or theft. In questions of finance, it suggests that investments in miniature works of art, *objets de vertu* and precious stones will be profitable.

In romantic or personal involvements, it shows a young girl sheltered from unwise influences.

When the question seems to have little connection with the symbolism of the Orchid – as in, say, matters concerning land and buildings – the purpose of this card is to direct attention away from the matter which is uppermost in the querent's mind, and suggests that there is another key to the solution.

See Readings:
Case 8

CHRYSANTHEMUM Chü 菊

37

Maturity
Contentment
Autumn

The Chinese regard the splendid Chrysanthemum as the symbol of the Sun, its golden petals radiating like sunbeams. Indeed, a stylized representation of the Chrysanthemum is used in the eastern world as the solar symbol. But it is its appropriateness for the Autumn season that is perhaps the most important meaning imparted by this card. A charming Chinese story tells of an Empress who dearly loved her husband. But she was growing older and her husband, as was customary, had decided to take another, younger, wife. Sadly, she asked him, 'What am I to you now that you have this lady to attend to you?' The Emperor smiled at her kindly, and replied gallantly, 'Like a chrysanthemum in Autumn'.

Chosen by a mature lady, this card reveals grace, charm, and kindness – qualities which this card lends to the Peacock (1 Bamboo) which also represents a matron. If the querent is obviously not intended, this combination of Chrysanthemum and Peacock will represent an older female relative, revealing her to be contented with her life and surrounded by the joys which a happy family brings.

The Autumn season is the time of harvest and wine making. Its ancient astrological symbol, a wine flask, signifies merriment, jollity, retirement and leisure.

The Chrysanthemum Guardian represents pleasure, social activities, holidays and entertainment. The most appropriate cards to be drawn to replace it are the Lute (4 Wan) and the West, which is the symbol of Autumn.

CENTRE CARD The Chrysanthemum Guardian at the Centre signifies leisure and entertainment; this is the clue to the way in which the querent's problem can be solved, while the card which is chosen to replace it will give a further hint. If the question asked concerns problems with personal relationships, then one must look at the amount of time devoted to leisure – it may be that the relationship as it exists does not give enough time to social activity. In financial matters, the Chrysanthemum Guardian suggests the entertainment industry would be the best field for speculation. When the matter under discussion concerns health, it indicates the need to release the pressure of work.

See Readings:
Case 12

BAMBOO

Chu 竹

The Bamboo has ten thousand uses, but short stems of bamboo are perhaps most familiar as the stems of the Chinese brush, used in China not only for painting, but for writing, too. Less familiar is the Chinese pen, a simple stem of bamboo with its end carved as a nib.

It is not so surprising, therefore, that the Bamboo Guardian is associated with writing, learning, and scholarship. Thus, it indicates help in the form of a communication or document, particularly the announcement of success in examinations.

The strength of the Bamboo, and the fact that it grows upright, are both symbols of the desired qualities in a young man, and it is sometimes held to be the model of virtuous behaviour. If the Pine (2 Circles) is drawn to replace the Bamboo Guardian, then it affirms the Pine's symbolism of a youth, but also affirms that the person is honest and true.

Even so, it can be considered an especially favourable sign when the card drawn to replace the Bamboo is, appropriately, one of the Bamboo suit, for then it underlines the sense of the written word in interpreting the cards. For example, with 5 Bamboo (Lotus, also meaning a child) it brings news of a birth, while with 6 Bamboo (Water, also meaning communication) it represents fortunate news with regards to a document. It frequently represents recovery from illness.

The other associated card is North, the direction of Winter. If this is drawn, it means that there will be help and protection through a difficult period.

CENTRE CARD When the Bamboo Guardian appears as the Centre card, it indicates that the answer to a particular question lies in a letter or document which will bring help and success. The extra card drawn to replace the Guardian card will reveal more about the nature of the communication. In matters of romance, it may refer to the marriage certificate; in matters of health, a medical prescription. If the querent has asked about a time factor, the Bamboo Guardian in the Centre position represents the following Winter, whatever time of the year the question was posed.

38

BAMBOO

Wisdom
Success in
examinations
Winter

See Readings:
Case 8

FISHERMAN

Yu 漁

39

FISHERMAN

Regeneration
Marriage

The Fisherman often depicted in Chinese miniatures represents the ancient philosopher Chiang T'ai Kung. He was discovered by King Wen of the Chou dynasty (who is attributed with the compilation of the commentaries to the I *Ching*). In discussion with the Fisherman, King Wen found him to be extremely wise, and took him to his court to be his prime minister. The Fisherman's philosophy was simple common sense; the ruler who got rich while his people suffered would not last long. The application to modern times is that good management leads to good working relationships which in turn brings prosperity to all. The Fisherman-philosopher is also renowned for his patience, perhaps a tactic he had learnt from his angling days.

The Fisherman is one of the two Guardians of Spring; it is associated with the direction East, the colour green, and the element Wood. Consequently, it is appropriate for this card to appear in the East sector, when it refers to the querent, or next to an East card, in which case it refers to someone (rather than a situation) very close. When the Fisherman Guardian appears, it often indicates that dealing with other people will proceed more smoothly by practising greater tolerance. It suggests that everything is proceeding along the right path, although this may not be evident at the moment.

If the Fisherman Guardian card appears in an unfavourable position, or the card drawn to replace the Fisherman seems to indicate adverse circumstances, then the Fisherman suggests that it would be wisest to wait until a more opportune moment arrives before taking any steps that may be necessary.

CENTRE CARD When the Fisherman appears at the Centre, this is a favourable reply to any queries regarding when or whether a specified event might happen, the response being that it will, and although later than expected, it will not be too late. For questions regarding marriage, it signifies a long engagement, but great happiness thereafter. When the question concerns finance, it suggests that long-term safe investments are better than risky speculations. In matters of health, it shows recovery after a long illness.

See Readings:
Case 4

WOODCUTTER

Ch'iao 樵

40

Abundance
Fertility

The Woodcutter chopping firewood is an allegorical representation of three of the five elements of Chinese philosophy; Fire and Wood are two of them, while Metal is represented by his axe. Fire is a crucial factor which controls the other two elements. Furthermore, in Mah Jongg, the Woodcutter represents the Summer, which is governed by the direction South and the element Fire. The meaning of this card is, therefore, much deeper than might be suspected from the picture of the simple Woodcutter.

The Fire represented by the Woodcutter Guardian reveals all the positive influences of vitality, drive, ambition and industry. It also shows someone holding the balance of power in a conflict. Here is the help needed to get a project underway. It reveals leadership, teamwork, and success through activity. The season Summer and the element Fire belong to the direction South, so it is appropriate for the Woodcutter to appear in the South, or with the South card, when it is a sign of great prosperity.

The appearance of the Woodcutter, although always a fortunate sign, is nevertheless an incentive to greater effort, for the rewards will be great – if not materially, then through promotion, greater recognition, or increased satisfaction. Indeed, if the Woodcutter appears in an unfavourable position, or with a card that has an adverse interpretation for the querent's present situation, its message is clearly that the querent should make every effort to hack a way clear through the present entanglements. This will be stressed if the Knot (8 Wan) or the Sword (2 Wan) are present anywhere.

CENTRE CARD The appearance of the Woodcutter is a favourable sign for all those about to embark on new ventures, especially if these require considerable planning and mental effort, Fire being the element of mind and intelligence.

Building and construction are particularly favoured if the House (5 Wan) is present in the spread.

In romantic matters, it suggests a very fiery relationship, involving a highly emotional and excitable partner. The card shows protection and recovery in cases of mental disorder or drug abuse.

See Readings:
Case 9

FARMER

Keng 耕

41

FARMER

Maturity
Promotion

Like the Chrysanthemum, the Farmer is another symbol of the Autumn. It signifies the tasks and toil of bringing in the harvest. Thus, the Farmer Guardian card indicates physical activity and arduous labour, but nevertheless labour which brings its own rich rewards.

The Autumn is associated with the West, the colour white, and the element Metal. Accordingly, it is appropriate for this card to appear with a West card or in the West sector. As West often refers to one's objectives, the Farmer shows that difficulties will be surmounted through physical effort. Note that this card stresses that bodily effort is required – this is not an oblique reference to perseverance or patience. It is a blunt command to get up and put one's back into a job.

The appearance of the Earth card (3 Wan) makes an obvious connection between the Farmer and the land, and can be interpreted at its face value for those who have land or are considering buying it; it might also refer to a legacy involving land ready for development.

Broadly speaking, however, the Farmer represents physical effort, a meaning underlined when Jade (4 Circles) or the Insect (7 Circles) appears in the spread.

CENTRE CARD The Farmer in the Centre position reveals success through physical effort. With cards which are favourable to the querent's present situation, the Farmer shows increasing benefits. Even if the card drawn to replace the Farmer in the Centre position seems adverse, the response signals that determined effort will continue to bring great rewards to the querent.

When the reading is a general one, the replacement card is an indication of where and how one's activity should be best directed – and it is worth emphasizing that it is physical effort which is demanded, not mental.

If the question concerns romance, the Farmer symbolizes a partner whose passions are basic and earthy, rather than genteel. If financial problems are uppermost, the answer lies in land or labour, as these will bring prosperity. For those who enquire about health, more exercise will improve the constitution.

See Readings:
Case 9

SCHOLAR

Tu 讀

The Scholar above all distinction is the sage Confucius, who begins his great work, the *Analects*, with the words: 'Study and practice – what could give greater pleasure?' The Scholar shown here is carrying a fly-whisk, which Taoist philosophers would wave to emphasize certain points during their discussions.

This card is associated with Winter, a time when there is little that can be successfully achieved outdoors: farming, hunting, and building must all wait for the better weather. During this fallow period, however, those of a cultured mind can turn their attentions to the creation of works of literary or artistic merit. For the manual worker, the Scholar stresses that paperwork must not be neglected.

The Scholar and the Bamboo Guardians both pertain to the North, the colour black, and the element Water (represented by 6 Bamboo). Water itself symbolizes communication – either through speech, literature, or travel – but when the Scholar Guardian appears, it is the teaching and learning aspect of communication which is emphasized. Thus the appearance of this card is a good sign for all those connected with counselling and education. If the Scholar appears in the North it indicates literary and scholarly merit, success in examinations, and recognition in the educational fields. Those who believe that their practical experience is sufficient for their success are warned that they may be putting themselves at a disadvantage because their theoretical knowledge is insufficient.

The Scholar often stresses the need to attend to correspondence, particularly if the Pine (2 Circles), representing ink, is close by. A spread which contains a high proportion of Bamboo suit cards also underlines the importance of the written word.

CENTRE CARD The Scholar promises great merit to the studious. Those wishing to know about their romantic prospects will find success with a partner who is quiet and studious. To those involved in legal and financial problems, there will be success when pertinent documents have been carefully researched. Quiet rest is advised to those who are concerned about health.

42

SCHOLAR

Prudence
Reserves

See Readings:
Case 11

SAMPLE
READINGS

十二算命法

Putting Questions to the Oracle

Most people approaching the Mah Jongg oracle for the first time tend to do so out of curiosity, without a definite question in mind. Only a general reading is expected; in other words, the querent is really asking, 'What do the next twelve months have in store for me?'

Then those who are more familiar with the oracle frequently have a particular problem for which advice is sought, but for personal reasons, this may not be stated aloud. When this is the case, the diviner should examine the Centre card carefully, as it often reveals the nature of the problem. When the Centre card does not immediately relate to the unspoken question, it may nevertheless be a key to its solution. The form of such questions is usually indefinite, for example: 'How am I going to sort out my emotional involvement?'

Sometimes the querent has a specific problem for which a precise answer is sought. In such cases, it is best to state the question aloud, so that the diviner can elicit the most relevant meanings of the Mah Jongg cards which appear. Questions of this nature need to be explicitly framed; for example: 'When can I expect the will to be proved?'

Whatever the question, they can nearly always be put into one of twelve categories which Chinese diviners call the twelve 'palaces'. Their names, and the subjects they cover are:

1. Fate: the course of life generally
2. Parents: including older relatives
3. Virtue: luck and happiness
4. Estate: real estate, land, possessions
5. Official: referring to career and promotion
6. Servants: and employees

7. Travel: moving house, living abroad
8. Sickness: and health
9. Wealth: money, investments
10. Sons: daughters, and younger relatives
11. Spouse: marriage and romance
12. Kindred: relatives of the same generation, and friends; the departed, the occult

It is good working practice to analyze the question before commencing the reading, and to decide into which category the question falls. Obviously, questions such as, 'Is my lover faithful?', 'Am I likely to marry during the coming year?', 'Which of the two should I choose?', 'Will my girlfriend wait for me while I go away?' all belong to the eleventh palace, Spouse. But a question of the type, 'Will my position improve during the coming year?', might seem to be a general enquiry (the first palace). The diviner, however, will need to know what the querent means by 'position' since this could be a specific question about career, finances, health, or romance. Knowing the appropriate palace helps the diviner to decide what aspect of the card's symbolism is most pertinent at that moment.

The final section of this book gives twelve examples of readings, one for each of the twelve palaces. Study these sample readings carefully, as they show how the diviner can follow the course of events from the first card to the last. Note how subtle changes of interpretation are revealed by the positioning of a particular card, its relationship to other cards in the group, and above all, with reference to the querent's own individuality. Thus, though the number of possible arrangements of the 144 cards may in theory be limited, the great variety of conditions which have brought the querent to the oracle means that no two readings will ever be the same!

77

Case I   (Fate)

Querent: John, 19, unemployed but skilled, living in a different city to his girlfriend. John admitted to having a specific question, but did not voice it.

The Centre card is the Tortoise (7 Bamboo), an indication of slow progress, but eventual success by using wisdom and experience. John must understand that the better things in life need time to fulfil.

The three Mah Jongg cards in the East sector which represents the querent, are an outstanding example of a group of Mah Jongg cards taken together revealing more than the individual components. The first card, the Peach (6 Circles), is a sign of a young girl; as it obviously does not relate immediately to the querent,

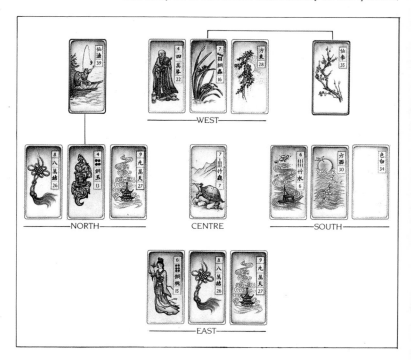

it must have some other significance. In the first position, as here, it might have signalled the querent's interest in art and painting, but the other two cards in this row reveal more of the situation. The third card in the row is 9 Wan, Heaven (the right-hand cards in the East and West rows are turned over before the middle ones), which signifies religious rites and ceremonies, while the second 'inner character' card is the Knot (8 Wan). Is John thinking of his girlfriend, and wondering whether he should 'tie the knot' in Church?

Proceeding to the South, the near future arising out of the present, we see Water (6 Bamboo) indicating travel and correspondence. Next is West, the objective, and thirdly, White, the blank card. This would seem to indicate that travel and correspondence are necessary for John to obtain his objective, while the White card emphasizes the need for important correspondence and documents. What obstacles stand in his way?

In the West, the objective sector, the Lute (4 Wan) representing leisure and enjoyment, reveals a too carefree attitude to life which is achieving nothing and wasting everything. The other obstacle is shown by the conflict of East, representing the Self, being in the West. John is his own worst enemy; self-discipline is needed. The answer to his problem is shown by the Insect (7 Circles), the symbol of activity and business. Furthermore, the Insect card is protected by the Guardian of the Plum Blossom, the symbol of youthful romance. Once John has got even an insignificant job, his problems will be cleared away, and relationships with his girlfriend will become easier.

In the North, the Knot (8 Wan) appears again, followed by Jade (4 Circles) and Heaven (9 Wan) for a second time. Another Guardian card appears – the Fisherman, signifying marriage. The Knot and Heaven being repeated so dramatically in the final sector brings the reading to a full circle, and the question of marriage returns again. But the Guardian of marriage is attached to Jade (4 Circles), symbolizing reward for effort. The message is clear: the knot will eventually be tied; John's search for better employment will be successful, after which the prospective marriage will be on a happier and surer foundation.

Case 2   (Parents)

Querent: Alice came to England from Eastern Europe many years ago. She wanted to know whether she would see her parents again.

The Centre card is the Insect (7 Circles), the sign of activity, and indicates that much work will have to be done before Alice can achieve success.

Turning to the personality reading, in the East sector of the spread, the Unicorn (9 Circles) in the first place reveals someone with the ability to look ahead; someone, too, who has the knack of being able to see through deceit. The Dragon (5 Circles) shows that she is gifted, and that she is likely to succeed in what she puts her mind to. The Jade (4 Circles) in the 'hidden'

————WEST————

————NORTH————

CENTRE

————SOUTH————

————EAST————

position reveals her to be a person of sound moral values herself, although she does not preach at others who do not share her high standards.

In the South, the Lotus (5 Bamboo), symbolized by a child, shows Alice thinking of her own childhood; a recent experience has triggered off a longing for her to be reunited with her parents. The Carp (4 Bamboo) reveals a long journey ahead; but it also indicates patience and perseverance. Another watery sign, the Willow (9 Bamboo) is next to it; but it is not a favourable sign in the South sector. Rather, it indicates that there are many difficulties ahead, and a careless overlooking of some essential detail will cause delays.

In the West, which reveals the obstacles to success and how they can be overcome, the first card turned is the White, or blank, card. This might be taken, on the surface, to mean the administrative documents which have to be put in order. Heaven (9 Wan) may refer to the end of one great period in Alice's life, but the two cards together have a much deeper and sadder meaning. The White and the Heaven card reveal that Alice is hiding her fear that she might never see her parents before they pass away, and for them, time is getting short. The solution lies in the middle card. Entering (1 Wan), a door opening, which provides the opportunities for Alice.

In the North sector we see Alice represented by the East card, in conflict with officialdom in the shape of the Tiger (8 Circles). But the Pearl (1 Circles) in the final place shows Alice succeeding – although not in the immediate future.

Although this reading does not show Alice meeting her parents yet, instead it appraises her of the many difficulties she is going to face. Indeed, the oracle is really telling her that her problems ahead are greater than she may have supposed, but they are not insurmountable. Administrative delays will be many, and though her meeting does not appear to be taking place within the year, the final preparations will be under consideration.

Case 3 (Virtue)

Querent: Barry, a regular gambler, wanted to know 'what his luck was like'.

With Centre as the Centre card, there is an indication of great fortune. It would, however, be irresponsible to tell a gambler that he was due to make his fortune, for gamblers are by nature over-optimistic, and the assurance of great dividends inevitably leads the gambler into rash speculation. The diviner must therefore use considerable discretion in the way that the interpretation is phrased.

In the East, representing the querent, the Willow (9 Bamboo) shows flexibility, and an unwillingness to face up to confrontation – or even reality. The Tortoise

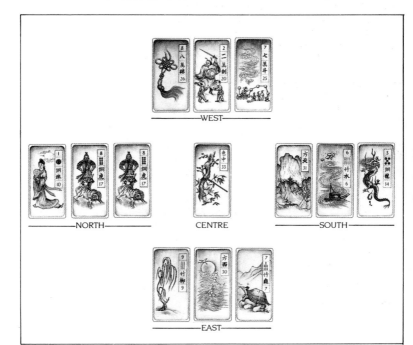

(7 Bamboo) shows dissatisfaction with the present circumstances, which appear to have been stagnating. Perhaps the root of Barry's insecurity can be found in the second card – the deeper side of the personality – which in this instance is West. West and East are equal and opposite partners; Barry would be happier if there were someone else to share his life.

In the South sector, the first card to appear is North – another card in its opposite place, and here representing recent losses. Water (6 Bamboo) shows that Barry will soon be making a journey, after which the Dragon (5 Circles) signifies a stroke of good fortune.

In the West, showing the obstacles to success and happiness, and the best way in which these can be overcome, there is a Knot (8 Wan) revealing inner anxieties, while the Seven Stars (7 Wan), indicating dreams and imagination, suggest that Barry is not coming to terms with reality; that he has too many fantasies, and lacks determination. The solution, shown by the Sword (2 Wan), is to cut through the Knot – in that he must face up to the problems which he has allowed to accumulate, and put his affairs in order.

In the North, the Pearl (1 Circles) reveals some financial successes eventually but, unfortunately, there are danger signs with the Tiger (8 Circles) in the eleventh position, showing conflict with authority. The repetition of this card in the twelfth position stresses the gravity of the circumstances which have led to this personal conflict.

Gamblers have their strokes of luck, and their misfortunes. This reading is full of the uncertainties of a gambler's life. Barry wanted to know what his luck was like; the signs are that he will get the big win that he wanted, but at considerable cost. It appears that in trying to repeat, or increase, an initial success he loses more than he had to start with. The oracle is not fatalistic; these are warning signs only. It is up to Barry to put his life in order.

Case 4 (Estate)

Querent: A lady approaching retirement age, who wonders whether she ought to move, or stay in the house where she has lived for the past twenty-five years. No further information was forthcoming, and she did not say whether her husband was still alive.

The Centre card is the Toad (3 Bamboo), the symbol of medicine and health. Consequently, it reveals that the key factor in making a decision whether to move or stay should not be the financial advantages, or family ties, or the benefits of improved scenery, but principally the consideration of convenience for someone in their later years. Whether it will be easy for an elderly person to get about, whether a doctor is within reach,

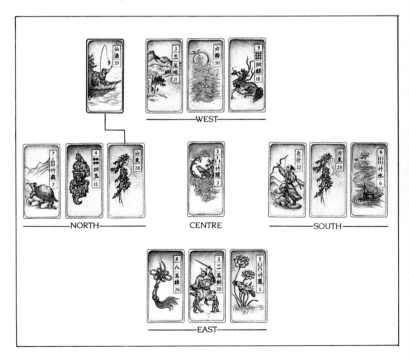

and whether shops and other amenities are readily available are all matters which must be borne in mind.

The lady's present quandary is shown by the cards in the East sector: the Knot (8 Wan), the Sword (2 Wan) in the second or 'hidden' place, and the Lotus (5 Bamboo). These three cards form an interesting group. Outwardly, she admits to her anxieties (the Knot), and probably discusses her problems with friends and others at every opportunity. For her, moving would mean a new life (the Lotus) and she worries about the uncertainty of whether to carry on peacefully in her familiar surroundings, or whether she feels herself capable of pulling up roots. Secretly, she longs to do this, as evidenced by the Sword with which she wants to cut the binding ties.

Arising from her immediate situation, the South cards show Commence (the Green character card), followed by East, which represents the querent, and Water (6 Wan), the sign of travel and communication. All this suggests that by all means the querent should go ahead and make enquiries, and that every effort to find the ideal location should be done sooner rather than later.

The obstacles which stand in her way are shown by the Earth (3 Wan) and the Unicorn (9 Circles). The Earth reveals the comforting stability of being in her present familiar surroundings; the Unicorn her looking apprehensively ahead and seeing all kinds of difficulties. The answer lies in West, appearing in its correct place, the West sector. In this particular instance, the relevance is very marked, since West is the direction attributed to Autumn and retirement.

The North has the Tortoise (7 Bamboo) in its own locality, which shows slow but fortunate progress; Jade (4 Circles) reveals objectives attained after hard work, while the Fisherman, the Guardian of Spring, is protecting the querent (East) in the final position. This shows that after taking health into consideration, the querent will be happy in a new location.

Case 5 (Official)

Querent: Shelley, in her late teens. She sat for the reading with her mother, as 'there was something important' they needed to know. The ladies did not give any indication of the nature of the problem, but the fact that the mother was anxious to sit in on the reading meant that this was something more far-reaching than the usual teenage romance.

The Centre card was the Knot (8 Wan) which immediately confirmed the seriousness of the problem, and one which the family did not seem confident enough to tackle without advice or encouragement from an unbiased bystander.

The personality cards show East in the first place, indicating someone with great self-assurance; the

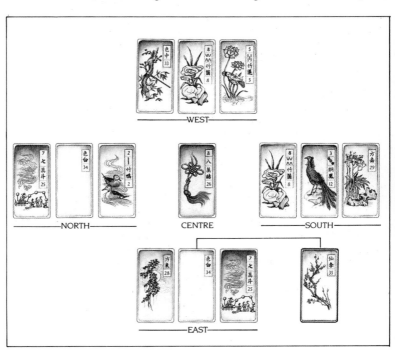

Seven Stars (7 Wan) show that this person has high ideals and ambitions, and a great deal of imagination. However, in the hidden part of the personality, there is an unknown quantity revealed by the White card. Furthermore, this secret aspect of Shelley's personal life is protected by the Plum Blossom Guardian, who looks after lovers. Shelley seems to have a deep, hidden, love which is a great secret.

In the South, the first card, showing the development of the present situation, is the Mushroom (8 Bamboo). This reveals a curious incident, some bizarre or eccentric event has happened which nevertheless has given Shelley considerable pleasure, as evinced by the Phoenix (3 Circles), the symbol of joy. It has brought Shelley success and excitement, shown by the South card being in its proper place – in the South.

But what is it that Shelley wants? And what stands in her way? First of all, there is her present driving ambition (we saw the East in the first place, coupled with the Seven Stars); the arrow striking its target, shown by the Centre, seems to suggest that Shelley may be putting her ambitions ahead of practicality. At the other side of the West sector is the Lotus (5 Bamboo) which sometimes represents a baby. The reappearance of the Mushroom (8 Bamboo) suggests that the solution lies in the unusual event encountered in the South sector.

Then, turning to the end result in the North sector, we see Shelley's ambitions, the Seven Stars (7 Wan) shining in the Winter sky. The White card reappears, followed by the Duck (2 Bamboo), revealing a happy partnership as the end result.

Shelley had been offered a theatrical engagement, which would have been the fulfilment of a great ambition. Unfortunately, she was also the unmarried mother of a beautiful baby, which she would have to leave in her own mother's care if she took the opportunity.

Case 6 (Servants)

Querent: Gentleman, early forties, on holiday in London. He wanted to know whether he was taking the right approach regarding the development of his business. This was an extremely intriguing reading, and one which showed that one should never be afraid of relaying what the Mah Jongg oracle has to say, even though the interpretation may go contrary to the diviner's intuition.

The Centre card is West, which means both the querent's objectives, and a partnership. As the querent had asked me about business prospects, I wondered whether this represented his new business arrangements, but confined myself to telling him that this card represented a successful partnership.

WEST

NORTH

CENTRE

SOUTH

EAST

In the East, representing the querent, Jade (4 Circles) appeared first, indicating a capacity for hard work, especially with regards to projects which are going to take a long time to perfect. The Toad (3 Bamboo) represents an interest, and possibly a career, in medicine, herbalism, and pharmaceuticals. The second card is the Lute (4 Wan), representing a love of music; being the hidden part of the character it may indicate that the querent would perhaps have liked to have made music his chosen career.

In the South, arising out of the present circumstances, is the Duck (2 Bamboo) which is an immediate reminder of the partnership shown by West in the Centre position. The Phoenix (3 Circles), indicating happiness, shows that this partnership will bring considerable happiness and fortune. Water (6 Bamboo) was apparently self-explanatory, knowing that the querent was a visitor to England. However, it transpired that this card had a further meaning which was overlooked at the time.

In the West, the obstacles to the project are Earth (3 Wan) – indicating that the present location may have been unsuitable – and the Pearl (1 Circles), which in financial considerations often shows difficulty in making funds available. The Lute (4 Wan), representing an interest in music, is an indication of a course of action which will be beneficial.

The end result, shown in the North sector, reveals the querent in person, by the repetition of the Toad (3 Bamboo) card, followed by the Mushroom (8 Bamboo), a sign of something unusual, with South, indicating complete success, in the final position.

The querent was extremely pleased with this reading, and pointed out that his holiday was in fact his honeymoon – the West, the Duck (2 Bamboo), and the Phoenix (3 Circles) all pointed to this – while in his profession as a medical practitioner he was very keen on using music therapeutically.

| # Case 7 (Travel)

Querent: a lady in her mid-thirties. This proved to be a highly interesting spread, because the querent was quite happy to accept the interpretation of the first ten cards as they were read. Then, suddenly, the last three cards seemed to contradict all that had been said before. Frankly, I was puzzled, but the querent was perfectly satisfied, however, and was able to give a simple explanation for the apparent discrepancy.

The querent wanted to enquire about travel, but did not expand on the question before the reading.

The Centre card is the Sword (2 Wan) indicating that the querent is having to face up to a situation where something has to be sacrificed in order to progress. In the East, describing the querent, there is Water (6

————WEST————

————NORTH————

CENTRE

————SOUTH————

————EAST————

Bamboo), which shows intelligence and communication, and as the question concerned travel, it may be assumed that this is the key factor to the problem. In the third place, there is the Insect (7 Circles), which shows hard work – but work which is performed to complete some immediate objective, rather than a long-term project. The middle card, the Duck (2 Bamboo) shows that long-standing partnerships take second place in this lady's life.

Now moving to the South sector, which relates to events arising out of the present, we see the Centre, showing achievement of objectives, and Entering (1 Wan), revealing new opportunities. It appears that this is a career lady who has recently received, or is about to get, promotion. This is emphasized by the next card being South, in its own sector, a sure indication of prosperity and success.

The obstacles in her path are the Pine (2 Circles) and the House (5 Wan). The Pine represents a younger male, and the House may be her own house, or some institution which is acting as a brake to her ambitions. But the way out is the green Commence; she must go ahead and do what she wants to do, despite her misgivings. As she asked about travel, here is the answer: 'Go'.

But in the North sector we find Heaven (9 Wan), meaning the end of a cycle. This is followed by the Lute (4 Wan), meaning leisure, and the Peach (6 Circles), which represents extravagance. Could it be that after having been promoted, and taken the decisive step to leave everything behind her, she then decides to give up her career? Well, not entirely! The lady admitted that she was a travel courier, divorced, with a son whom she intended to place at a boarding school, since she had recently been promoted to a residential position abroad. Her work, being seasonal, entitled her to long vacations which she usually spent in the Bahamas.

Case 8 (Sickness)

Querent: Stanley, retired, is anxious about his health, and worried about the outcome of an operation.

The Mushroom (8 Bamboo), the sign of the uncommon, appearing in the Centre position suggests that more lies behind the querent's problem than a simple regard for his health, and the success of the forthcoming operation. The querent agreed that his health was central to the problem, but there were several other matters – family business, finances, as well as his own personal circumstances – all of which were converging onto his present situation. He then confided that he thought his family couldn't wait to get rid of him, but did not give the reason.

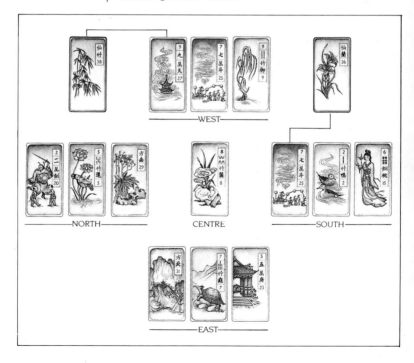

In the East, his personality is revealed by the North card as a stern disciplinarian. The House (5 Wan) shows him holding a tight rein on the management of the family home. The Tortoise (7 Bamboo), symbolizing thought, wisdom and experience, appears as the hidden part of his personality, indicating someone who ponders deeply before taking action. This possibly accounts for his seemingly suspicious nature, although it may have been experience which has made him unduly cynical.

In the South, the Orchid Guardian protects his hopes, shown by the Seven Stars (7 Wan). There is help at hand to enable him to realize his current ambitions. This encouraging sign is followed by the Duck (2 Bamboo), the symbol of a partnership or marriage, and the Peach (6 Circles), a young girl. This seemed to indicate a marriage or business partnership with a young lady in the driving seat, something which Stanley showed great interest in.

Obstacles were shown by the Willow (9 Bamboo), which, in an unfavourable position, is often a sign that important matters keep getting deferred – in this case, it appears, the important operation. Basically, however, it was the Heaven (9 Wan) card, revealing the end of a period of life, which may have been the greater obstacle. This card, however, is protected by the Bamboo Guardian – Stanley need have no fears of the operation. Indeed, his aspirations (the Seven Stars (7 Wan) protected by the Orchid Guardian in the South sector) are shown as the solution to his present problems as they appear again in the West.

The Sword (2 Wan) in the North sector cuts away the past, leaving Stanley to begin a new life, shown by the Lotus (5 Bamboo), while the South card, in the last position, promises Stanley happiness, contentment, and prosperity.

I never did discover, although I had my own thoughts on the matter, whether it was the business partnership or prospect of a second marriage which had so interested Stanley.

Case 9 (Wealth)

Querent: Tommy, who admits to being in his 'mid-forties' is a well-known entertainer. His question, 'Will I be rich?' was posed partly in jest, but reflected an inner insecurity due to the precarious nature of his profession.

The Pearl (1 Circles) in the Centre position answers the question unequivocally; placed in this position it is the symbol of riches.

In the East, the cards revealing the querent's personality begin with the Woodcutter, Guardian card of Summer, which was replaced by the Centre. Here is someone ambitious, perhaps giving the impression of being self-centred, but this may be due to the demands of his professional act of being a media

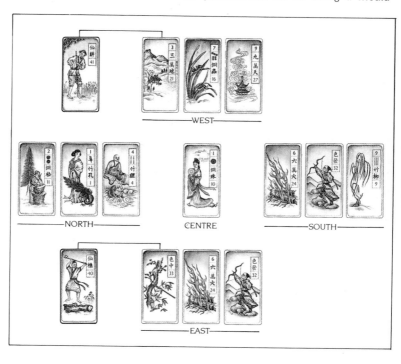

personality. Tommy's extroversion and enthusiastic nature is also revealed by the green Commence card which provides much of the driving power. There is also Fire (6 Wan) as the inner self; again this provides stimulus, but as Fire is also the sign of intelligence, it may be that there is a wish to do something more intellectually demanding than he does — very success-fully — at the moment.

In the South side of the spread, revealing the continuation of the present situation, Fire (6 Wan) and Commence appear again, showing that Tommy is at the moment in such popular demand that there is scarcely any time to attend to other matters. Every waking moment seems to be taken up by the demands of the current programme. But the situation is only temporary; in three months' time, shown by the Willow (9 Bamboo) in the sixth position, there will be a welcome respite from the present hectic activity.

In the West, which represents the obstacles to success, the Guardian of Autumn, the Farmer, has been replaced by Earth (3 Wan). This is an extraordinary combination, for it indicates both physical labour and land, neither of which have any relevance to Tommy's present circumstances. The other obstacle is Heaven (9 Wan), which can be interpreted as meditation, or the end of an era. The middle card of the three is the Insect (7 Circles), which represents busy activity. But Tommy himself admitted that after the current season, he would have plenty of time to think about what he wanted to do in life, and getting down to doing some actual labouring — possibly gardening — would be extremely beneficial for his health after the continual nervous strain of the last few months. The Insect would show Tommy returning to his professional career after a much needed break.

But it would appear that the intervening time would give him an opportunity to spend time peacefully with his family, shown in the North sector by the Pine (2 Circles), a young man, the Peacock (1 Bamboo), a mature lady, and the Carp (4 Bamboo), a long life.

Case 10 (Sons)

Querent: Grace is the mother of Sylvia who has just become engaged. Grace is not entirely happy about this; has Sylvia made the right choice?

The Centre card is the Pine (2 Circles) which represents a young man; in the reading, the central figure is not the querent, Grace, nor her daughter Sylvia, but Sylvia's fiancé. The Pine shows a young man who is more of a thinker than a practical person (he was a student at the time) and Sylvia's parents are worried about his prospects.

Because the querent is asking about another person, the cards in the East refer more to Grace's present circumstances, rather than to her personality. In the

WEST

NORTH

CENTRE

SOUTH

EAST

first position there is a door about to be opened (Entering, 1 Wan), in the ideal position for the start of any new venture, which the engagement is. The Knot (8 Wan) represent's Grace's apprehensions, while in the second position, hidden from the querent, is the Phoenix (3 Circles). The Phoenix is a sign of joy and happiness, and only appears in the reign of a good emperor. This therefore represents happiness which Grace has not yet been able to recognize.

Turning to the South, which shows the development of the present situation, there is the Peach (6 Circles) which obviously represents the young girl, Sylvia. Next to Sylvia is the House (5 Wan), bringing the prospect of a new home closer, because being in the South, it is in a favourable situation. This is followed by the Unicorn (9 Circles), which reveals foresight and an ability to plan ahead.

What are the obstacles – or in this particular case, what is at the root of Grace's objection? First of all, the Insect (7 Circles) represents busy activity and work. Perhaps Grace is fearful of the amount of work involved in preparing for the wedding, but more likely she is unhappy about the fact that the fiancé does not yet have any employment. Then there is the Dragon (5 Circles), which normally shows wealth and good luck, but in an unfavourable position shows the reverse – money being spent. The solution lies in the Peacock (1 Bamboo), which is the sign of a mature lady: Grace herself. Once Grace accepts the fact that most couples begin their lives together in circumstances which are far from ideal, she will find that her objections are really everyday practical obstacles which will always be present.

The Carp (4 Bamboo) in the North, showing slow developments, indicates a longer engagement than anticipated. But the Pine (2 Circles), Sylvia's fiancé again, with West, indicating partnership, in the final position reveals that they will indeed marry eventually.

Case II   (Spouse)

Querent: Jane was a lady in her late thirties; her problem was clear and precise — what were her marriage prospects? Sadly, without the intermediary of the Mah Jongg oracle, it would have been difficult to answer her question without either being truthful and unkind, or tactful to the point of mendacity. She was a hard-working lady, in public service, and probably with considerable savings, but her physical attractiveness was not immediately evident, and her social graces were few.

The Centre card is the Tortoise (7 Bamboo), which reveals general dissatisfaction with the present situation. But although the tortoise moves slowly, it nevertheless reaches its goal in the end, after experience and wisdom have been gained.

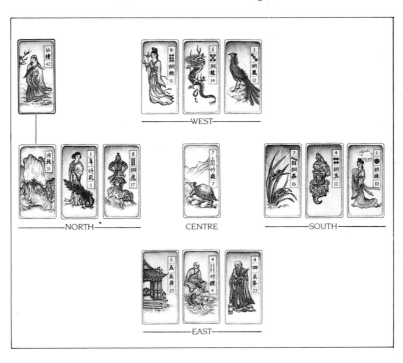

The House (5 Wan) shows that Jane puts great store by a stable home life, and the Lute (4 Wan) a love of music which is put into practice. (She admitted playing the piano.) The Carp (4 Bamboo), being the middle card of the personality row, shows a sound physical constitution and a long life.

In the South, the Insect (7 Circles) and the Jade (4 Circles) indicate that she is an extremely busy person, working on several levels. Indeed, it might even be that she overworks herself, to the exclusion of her social life. This activity may be in part a compensation for her loneliness, but – revealed by the Pearl (1 Circles) in the South – it will bring her both recognition and promotion in her career. Perhaps, too, she is concerned about salting money away for her old age.

But what are the obstacles to Jane's marriage prospects? The Peach (6 Circles) represents a beautiful young girl – which Jane clearly isn't, although there is a lot which she could do to improve her physical attractiveness. The Phoenix (3 Circles) reveals the joy which is lacking from her life. The answer lies in the Dragon (5 Circles), which is a way of telling Jane to be a little more extrovert, to socialize, and perhaps encourage her to splash out a bit.

The outcome, as revealed in the North, shows North with the Scholar Guardian. North is in its proper place, and both the Scholar and North are attributes of Winter. This is followed by the Peacock (1 Bamboo), the mature lady, and the Tiger (8 Circles), an older man, or man in uniform. For Jane this final row is an extremely happy combination, for it represents a mature couple, preceded by the Guardian Scholar giving advice.

The answer seems to be for Jane to pay greater attention to her appearance, to widen the circle of her activities and acquaintances, and to realize that there is more to life than just work. Then, her prospects of marriage may not be too remote after all.

Case 12 (Kindred)

Querent: Bella wished to know whether she should practise and develop her clairvoyant powers. This vivacious youngish (divorced) lady had a keen interest in occult matters, and was conversant with elementary astrological principles, and the Tarot. Bella had also toyed with the I Ching, but found it too academic for her, feeling herself drawn instead to something more demonstrable, such as spiritualism and the planchette. She was sure that if she had psychic powers, the Mah Jongg oracle would pick this up, and respond accordingly. All this information was freely volunteered before the reading began, which frankly made an impartial interpretation very difficult. Fortunately, her choice of cards, especially the final ones, allowed the oracle to speak for itself, and her own judgement to be guided through the interpretation of the cards.

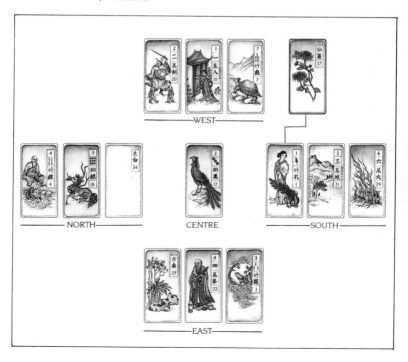

First, the Phoenix (3 Circles) in the Centre position indicates a favourable response to her enquiry, since the Phoenix only appears during the reign of a beneficent emperor. This was an encouraging sign.

In the East sector, Bella's warm and ebullient personality is shown by the South, while the Toad (3 Bamboo) revealed an • interest in herbalism and alternative medicine. In the second place, the hidden side of her nature, the Lute (4 Wan) revealed a fondness for music – she admitted cherishing an ambition to be an opera singer.

Turning to the South sector, and events arising out of the present situation, we see the Chrysanthemum Guardian protecting the Peacock (1 Bamboo), which here refers to the querent. Earth (3 Wan) appeared next, which suggested that Bella might be considering moving to another location, somewhere with different surroundings. This was followed by Fire (6 Wan), which in the South warns against mental exhaustion.

In the West, the problems she would have to face were shown first by the Sword (2 Wan), indicating that in order to make progress, she would have to make some personal sacrifice, since her aims were not compatible with her present situation. (She admitted that her landlady did not approve of her interest in the occult.) Also, her impatience was a fault, the Tortoise (7 Bamboo) teaching that time and experience bring understanding. But the door to further knowledge is waiting to be opened, as revealed by the middle card, Entering (1 Wan).

The Carp (4 Bamboo) again suggests that if she can develop an inner calmness it will bring the clairvoyant gifts of the Unicorn (9 Circles) which she seeks. Finally, in the last position, the White card is one of the Three Blessings, and a sign of the mystic adept.

Abridged Rules for Playing Mah Jongg

The Mah Jongg oracle cards are an exact match of traditional Mah Jongg tiles, and it is therefore possible to play the game of Mah Jongg with them. The rules vary slightly, especially in the matter of scoring, from one community to another, and it is therefore essential that players agree on 'house rules' before play commences. The following is a brief outline of the standard method of play.

There should be four players; for friendly games three or even two players are possible.

Places at the table are decided; players are known as East, South, West and North; South sits on East's right and East deals. East remains dealer until losing, when the deal passes to South (who is then called East) and so continues. Play proceeds anti-clockwise.

East deals each player thirteen cards, self first (four at a time, plus an extra one), and then a fourteenth card to self.

The object is to make a 'hand' of four sets of three cards, plus a matching pair. Certain combinations of sets produce higher and higher scores, but the winner of the round is the first one to make the complete hand, whatever the score may be. The winner keeps all points; the other three players deduct the winner's points from their own scores.

A set may comprise three consecutive cards of the same suit (*chow*) or three identical suit or Honours cards (*pung*). Unless the dealer wins outright with all fourteen cards at once, one card is thrown out and another taken from the pack. Play then proceeds anti-clockwise.

However, if any player has two cards identical to the one discarded it may be called and the order of play broken. If a card is called, the calling player places the card, and the two others, face upwards on the table to make an 'exposed pung'. A set of three identical cards made by a player without having to call for another card is called a 'hidden pung'. Hidden pungs count for double the points of exposed pungs.

If a player has a hidden pung in the hand, and a fourth identical card is discarded, a 'kong' may be called. The four cards make an 'exposed kong'. On making a kong, the player must take an extra card, the four cards counting as one set; otherwise it would not be possible to make the required number of sets. For the same reason, an extra card must be taken when a hidden kong is made. The hidden kong has to be displayed – but is still counted as hidden, and differentiated from the exposed kong by the cards being placed criss-cross fashion. Exposed kongs count for double the points of hidden pungs, and hidden kongs double again.

If a Guardian is dealt, it is immediately placed down and an extra card taken. Guardians score points, but are not used for making sets.

As soon as a player has made four sets and a matching pair (two identical cards) play stops, and the points are calculated.

Scoring

For every chow:	0 points
For every exposed pung of 2–8 suit cards:	2 points
For every exposed pung of 1 or 9 suit cards:	4 points
For every exposed pung of Honours:	4 points
For every hidden pung:	double the above
For every kong:	double the points for pung
For every Guardian:	4 points

The following scores only apply to winning hands:

For winning:	32 points
If dealer wins:	double total score
All cards of one suit:	double total score
For a pung or kong of the player's own direction:	double total score
For a pung or kong of Fa, Chung, or Pai:	double total score for each pung or kong
All cards 1 or 9:	double total score
All Honours:	double total score
A Guardian for each season:	double total score

Further Reading

Other books by the author on related subjects include:
Fortune Telling by the Mah Jongg, Aquarian, Wellingborough
Chinese Astrology, Aquarian, Wellingborough
The Alternative I Ching, Aquarian, Wellingborough
Ming Shu – the Art and Practice of Chinese Astrology, Pagoda, London
Cast Your Own Chinese Horoscope, Pagoda, London

Acknowledgements

The author wishes to acknowledge his thanks to Richard L.H. Tsui, Diviner, Temple of Wong Tai Sin, Kowloon; the staff of the Department of Oriental Manuscripts and Printed Books, The British Library, London; and to Jo Logan and Bettina Lee of *Prediction* Magazine.

Eddison Sadd Editions acknowledge contributions from the following people:

Editorial Director
Ian Jackson

Creative Director
Nick Eddison

Designer and Illustrator
Amanda Barlow

Editor and Proofreader
Geraldine Christy

Calligrapher
Yat Yan Cheung

Production
Bob Towell